FROM THE BIBLE-TEACHING
CHARLES R. SW~~INDOLL~~

INSIGHT'S
NEW TESTAMENT
Handbook

A PRACTICAL LOOK AT EACH BOOK

INSIGHT FOR LIVING

INSIGHT'S NEW TESTAMENT HANDBOOK
A Practical Look at Each Book

From the Bible-Teaching Ministry of Charles R. Swindoll

Charles R. Swindoll has devoted his life to the clear, practical teaching and application of God's Word and His grace. A pastor at heart, Chuck has served as senior pastor to congregations in Texas, Massachusetts, and California. He currently pastors Stonebriar Community Church in Frisco, Texas, but Chuck's listening audience extends far beyond a local church body. As a leading program in Christian broadcasting, *Insight for Living* airs in major Christian radio markets around the world, reaching people groups in languages they can understand. Chuck's extensive writing ministry has also served the body of Christ worldwide and his leadership as president and now chancellor of Dallas Theological Seminary has helped prepare and equip a new generation for ministry. Chuck and Cynthia, his partner in life and ministry, have four grown children and ten grandchildren.

Original charts were taken from the following series:

God's Masterwork, Volume 4, Matthew through 1 Thessalonians
Copyright © 1982, 1997 by Charles R. Swindoll, Inc.

God's Masterwork, Volume 5, 2 Thessalonians through Revelation
Copyright © 1982, 1983, 1998 by Charles R. Swindoll, Inc.

Copyright © 2010 by Insight for Living and Charles R. Swindoll, Inc.

Published by
IFL Publishing House
A Division of Insight for Living
Post Office Box 251007
Plano, Texas 75025-1007

Writers: John Adair, Th.M., Ph.D., Dallas Theological Seminary
Derrick G. Jeter, Th.M., Dallas Theological Seminary
Barb Peil, M.A., Christian Education, Dallas Theological Seminary
Editor in Chief: Cynthia Swindoll, President, Insight for Living
Executive Vice President: Wayne Stiles, Th.M., D.Min., Dallas Theological Seminary
Theological Editors: John Adair, Th.M., Ph.D., Dallas Theological Seminary
Derrick G. Jeter, Th.M., Dallas Theological Seminary
Content Editor: Amy L. Snedaker, B.A., English, Rhodes College
Copy Editors: Jim Craft, M.A., English, Mississippi College
Kathryn Merritt, M.A., English, Hardin-Simmons University
Project Coordinator, Creative Ministries: Melanie Munnell, M.A., Humanities,
The University of Texas at Dallas
Project Coordinator, Communications: Sarah Magnoni, A.A.S., University of Wisconsin
Proofreader: Paula McCoy, B.A., English, Texas A&M University-Commerce
Cover Design: Kari Pratt, B.A., Commercial Art, Southwestern Oklahoma State University
Production Artist: Nancy Gustine, B.F.A, Advertising Art, University of North Texas
Cover Image: Wayne Stiles, Th.M., D.Min., Dallas Theological Seminary

ISBN: 978-1-57972-893-9
Printed in the United States of America

TABLE OF CONTENTS

THE GENERAL EPISTLES

THE APOCALYPSE

APPENDIXES

A NOTE FROM
CHUCK SWINDOLL

Don't you just love good music?

The great masters of classical music—you know their names, Bach, Beethoven, Handel, and Mozart—produced what we might call "weighty" music. It is impressive. It is timeless. It is noteworthy. In those qualities it reflects the glory of God. The beauty produced as instruments and voices work together in perfect harmony lead us to praise Him.

We might say the same about the New Testament. It is "weighty" because it is impressive, timeless, and noteworthy. As divine revelation, it reflects the glory of God. As the twenty-seven books of the New Testament work together proclaiming the good news about Jesus, they lead us to God in praise and adoration for His good work on our behalf.

The New Testament records a tantalizing rhythm throughout its pages, delivering an account of the life of Jesus Christ—His miraculous birth, His spotless life, His healing miracles, His sacrificial death, and His glorious resurrection. Jesus taught that "he who has seen Me has seen the Father" (John 14:9). By portraying Jesus, each book by each human author plays in harmony with the others to most clearly reveal the Father.

What more meaningful melody could we explore than that of the life and ministry of Jesus Christ? *Insight's New Testament Handbook: A Practical Look at Each Book* will guide you through your exploration and study of our Lord as He is presented in the New Testament. As an introduction and quick-reference to each of the Bible books from Matthew to Revelation, this handbook includes: the "who," "when," and "where"; discussions of major themes and life-application points;

and charts and maps to provide context for the New Testament as a whole. *Insight's New Testament Handbook* will prove a valuable resource in your personal Bible study or as a resource for leading groups through particular books of the New Testament.

We all love a good melody, and none has been better conceived and performed than the symphony of God's gracious plan of redemption through the sacrifice of His Son. I hope that this handbook will make that theme and so much else all-the-more-clear to you. And I pray that as you grow in your faith through your study of God's Word, your life will become your own song of praise to Him who is worthy. Sing well and sing out!

Charles R. Swindoll

WHAT MAKES THE NEW TESTAMENT NEW?

Kids aren't always the best theologians, but often they're the most entertaining ones. For example, a father asked his 4-year-old son what God looks like. Nicholas said, "Well, Jesus is God, so God looks like Jesus." "Wow," his dad responded, "a theologically astute answer, son!" "And Jesus looks like a ghost," Nicholas added.

Clearly, like many of us, Nicholas has come a long way in his theological understanding . . . and has a long way to go.

Comedian Bill Cosby has also had his share of deep theological conversations with children. He relates one he had with a young man named Max.

> "Do you know how God punished Adam and Eve for eating the apple?" I asked one small boy. . . .
>
> "Yeah," he replied. "God made 'em sit down and read the Bible."
>
> "Well, at *that* point, reading the Bible didn't take very long."
>
> "No, the Bible's a *big* book. They got 'em in church. I see 'em there all the time."
>
> "What I mean, Max, is that almost nothing had *happened* yet when they were in the Garden of Eden, so there was almost nothing to *put* in the Bible."
>
> "Maybe in *your* church," said Max.[1]

Max was right, of course—the Bible is a *big* book. Oh, it wasn't big when Adam and Eve were running around the garden. (Technically, there wasn't even a Bible then.) But by the time Max was old enough to run around the church, the Bible had become a very big book indeed. With the Old Testament's thirty-nine books and the New Testament's twenty-seven books, anyone sitting down to read the Bible might come to the same conclusion as Max did. Even without the New Testament, the Old Testament is big in itself. Why do we need a New Testament? And besides, what makes the New Testament new, anyway?

Three Reasons Why the New Testament Is New

For Max and for the rest of us if we're really honest, even the "New" Testament is old. The "newest" books in the New Testament, 1 John and Revelation, are almost two thousand years old! Calling the New Testament "new" sounds more like an oxymoron than a statement in fact. So, if the New Testament is thousands of years old, what makes it new? Three reasons answer this question.

Reason One: Historically, God Broke His Silence

When God told the Old Testament prophet Malachi to put down his pen after the final period, God decided He had said enough . . . at least for a time. For the next four hundred years, through the golden age of Greece with its great philosophers Socrates, Plato, and Aristotle and with the conquests of Alexander the Great, God uttered not a single new word. For four hundred years, through the flowering of Rome and the rise of Julius Caesar, Marc Antony, and Cicero, God remained mute. For four hundred years, through Antiochus IV Epiphanes and his desecration of God's temple in Jerusalem (as predicted in Daniel 11:30–32) and the Jewish revolt that followed it under the leadership of Judas Maccabeus (11:33–35), nary a peep was heard from God. For four hundred years the divine silence was deafening . . . until God dispatched the angel Gabriel to announce the birth of a new prophet—John the Baptizer—by quoting the last prophet, Malachi (Luke 1:11–17). And when John appeared on the scene and cried, "Repent, for the kingdom of heaven is at hand" (Matthew 3:2), the voice of God was heard anew.

Reason Two: Biblically, God Completed His Written Revelation

The Old Testament was God's incomplete revelation. In it we find the foreshadowing of biblical and historical events and promises made. But in the New Testament, we find the fulfillment of these foreshadows and promises. Malachi, writing under the inspiration of the Holy Spirit, foretold the coming of John the Baptist, saying, "Behold, I am going to send My messenger, and he will clear the way before Me" (Malachi 3:1). In the book of Matthew, the Holy Spirit recorded that John was "one crying in the wilderness, / 'Make ready the way of the Lord, / Make His paths straight!'" (Matthew 3:3). The prophet Isaiah predicted that a virgin girl would give birth to One called "God with us" (Isaiah 7:14). This came true when Gabriel announced to Joseph that his virgin fiancée would give birth to Immanuel (Matthew 1:20–23). These and myriad other foreshadows and promises find their fulfillment and meaning in God's final written revelation, the New Testament.

Reason Three: Theologically, God Did Something New

In the days of the Old Testament, God prescribed a set of laws which governed the relationship between Himself and sinful humanity. In those former times, sinful men and women were required to bring an animal sacrifice to the temple for atonement of their sins. The priest would, on their behalf, make an offering to God by killing the animal, its spilt blood representing the payment of sin so that the worshipper might receive forgiveness and live. The system of temple sacrifice was an act of grace on God's part, motivating and requiring an act of faith on the part of sinners. When Christ came, however, God transformed the obligations of grace, faith, sacrifice, and blood into something new. No longer would God make His home in the temple but would live among His people as divinity incarnate—as the God-man, Jesus (John 1:14). No longer would sinful humanity have to offer repeatedly a blemish-free lamb at the temple for the remission of sin, because God's perfect Lamb—Christ—offered Himself as our sacrifice once for all (10:17–18).

No longer would humanity have to carry the burdensome dread of death, because in Jesus's resurrection, spiritual death died (1 Corinthians 15:54–55). No longer would humanity be separated from God by religious rules. Now, free and unfettered access is available to all who, in faith, respond to Jesus's call to believe (Hebrews 10:19–22). This "new and living way," found in following Christ, finds its full expression in the old books of the New Testament.

How to Use This Handbook

When reading most books, you simply pick up the book and start reading the first page. You can do that with this one, of course, but *Insight's New Testament Handbook* is a little different. It is designed to be used as a resource when you study your Bible. As you read the New Testament, bring along this handbook. From information on authors and settings to summaries, themes, and charts, the information contained in this handbook will provide a helpful context for what you read in the New Testament. We hope you will find this resource to be a valuable addition to your ongoing study of God's Word.

INSIGHT'S
NEW TESTAMENT
Handbook

THE
GOSPELS

The Gospels record the ministry, death, and resurrection of Jesus Christ; however, they are not intended to be biographies of our Lord. Instead, the Gospels take on a more theological role, picking and choosing from over three years of Jesus's teaching and ministry to present four unique but complementary portraits of the Savior. Due to their exclusive focus on Jesus Christ, it has been said that the gospels of Matthew, Mark, Luke, and John are the four pillars on which the church stands.

MATTHEW

—❧❧❧—

Who Wrote the Book?

While Matthew did not sign his own name to "his" gospel, the early church uniformly attested to the apostle's authorship of the book. As early as AD 140, a Christian named Papias wrote that Matthew had compiled the sayings of the Lord in Hebrew (presumably before Matthew translated them into Greek for a larger audience).

Matthew's name appears in all the biblical lists of the twelve apostles, though Mark and Luke refer to him as Levi. His history as a tax collector distinguished him from the other apostles, and immediately after his call to follow Jesus—an event he recorded in Matthew 9:9—Matthew hosted a feast for Jesus in his home with an invitation list made up of Matthew's sinful friends. Apparently Matthew did not think it odd that Jesus and he would associate with the sinful and downtrodden of society.

Where Are We?

Matthew is the most Jewish-centric of the four gospels. The apostle regularly invoked the writings of the Old Testament prophets in an effort to illustrate Jesus's identity as Israel's long-awaited Messiah.

However, the gospel of Matthew has been notoriously difficult to date. Several factors speak to a date ranging from AD 60–65. First of all, the book makes no mention of the destruction of the temple, an event which occurred in AD 70. Such a cataclysmic event likely would have received some comment, particularly in a book so clearly influenced by Judaism. The largely Jewish character of the book also suggests it was written at a time when much of the evangelism by Christians was directed more exclusively at Jews, something that became less and less common as the decades passed. Finally, many scholars believe Mark to have been the first gospel composed, making it most probable that Matthew was written soon after.

Why Is Matthew so Important?

The apostle Matthew, a Jew himself, offered a decidedly Jewish perspective on the ministry of Jesus. He included more than fifty direct citations—and even more indirect allusions—from the Old Testament. This exceeds any of the other gospels and indicates that Matthew had the Jewish population in mind when he sat down to write. Matthew's extensive connections between Jesus and the Old Testament provide ample prophetic evidence for Jesus's ministry but also give contemporary readers a glimpse into how first-century readers approached the Old Testament with a Christ-centered mind-set.

In addition, Matthew's gospel answers the question on the mind of every Jewish reader: "If Jesus is the King of the Jews, then where is God's promised kingdom?" Matthew reveals that Jesus did offer the kingdom to Israel, but the offer was rejected (Matthew 4:17; 16:13–28; 21:42–43). God's primary work in the world is now accomplished through the building of Christ's church, after which Jesus will come again to earth and establish His kingdom—ruling the world from Israel.

What's the Big Idea?

Matthew wrote his account of Jesus's ministry to show that Jesus was and is indeed the King, Israel's long-awaited Messiah. He reflected this concern in his opening line, "The record of the genealogy of Jesus the Messiah, the son of David, the son of Abraham" (Matthew 1:1). From there, Matthew consistently took his readers back to the Old Testament, providing Old Testament testimony regarding the birth of Jesus, Bethlehem as the location of Jesus's birth, the flight to Egypt, Herod's slaughter of the infants, and the beginning of Jesus's ministry. In a world where many in the Jewish community had claimed the role of Messiah for themselves, Matthew's commitment to grounding the life of Jesus in the Old Testament raised Jesus above the multitude of these false messiahs. The apostle painted a portrait of our Lord that highlights His uniqueness among all others to ever walk this earth.

How Do I Apply This?

After enduring four hundred years of prophetic silence, God's people must have wondered whether or not He had deserted them. After centuries of regular communication from God, the people found themselves without a genuine prophet or spokesman for God. However, the ministries of John and Jesus reminded God's people that He had not forgotten them. God's silence during that period was merely a precursor to pulling the linchpin of His redemptive plan. God hadn't forgotten—He remembered His people. Matthew made that clear.

It was true then, and it is certainly true today. Do you ever feel as though God has deserted you or that He sits in silence in the face of your requests? As we read through the pages of Matthew, not only do we see Jesus Christ revealed as Israel's King and Messiah, but His coming to earth as God in the flesh reminds us of His deep love for us. Now resurrected and ascended, the Lord Jesus will always be with us, even to the end of time (Matthew 28:20).

Christ's commission to His followers is still His mandate to us today: "Make disciples of all the nations" (Matthew 28:19). Christ's work of building His church is the work He does through each of us.

MATTHEW

	Announcement and Arrival of the King	Proclamation and Reception of the King	Opposition and Rejection of the King	Resurrection and Triumph of the King
	Main Emphasis: His Credentials	**Main Emphasis: His Message**	**Main Emphasis: His Suffering and Death**	**Main Emphasis: His Conquest**
	Birth	Sermon on the Mount	Spread of opposition	God's power
	Baptism	Miracles	Preparation of disciples	Great Commission
	Temptation	Discourses	Final predictions	
		Parables	Crucifixion	
	CHAPTERS 1–4	*CHAPTERS 5–15*	*CHAPTERS 16–27*	*CHAPTER 28*
The King	His identity: Israel's promised King		His destiny: "Crucify Him!"	
Scope	Teaching the vast multitudes		Teaching the Twelve	
Location	Bethlehem and Nazareth	Ministry in Galilee	Ministry in Judea	
People's Reaction	Increased popularity		Increased hostility	
Theme	Jesus is the King, Israel's long-awaited Messiah.			
Key Verses	16:16–19; 28:18–20			
Christ in Matthew	Jesus, the Messiah, fulfills the prophecies, promises, types, and expectations of the Old Testament Scriptures (16:16–19; 28:18–20).			

MARK

—⚜—

Who Wrote the Book?

The Bible records more information about Mark than any of the other gospel writers aside from the apostle John. Luke mentioned Mark's name several times in Acts. A budding Jerusalem church met in his mother's home. Mark also started the first missionary journey with Paul and Barnabas but went home early, though he later traveled with Barnabas to Cyprus for more mission work. He became significant in the life of Paul, being one of the last people the apostle mentioned in his final letter (2 Timothy 4:11).

However, Mark's most significant personal connection was the one he had with Peter, who was likely Mark's source for the material in the gospel. Mark's mother's house was a regular enough stop for Peter that the servants recognized him by voice alone (Acts 12:12–14). And it appears that Mark was present at Gethsemane, a young man watching the proceedings from a safe distance (Mark 14:51–52), leading some scholars to believe the Last Supper took place in Mark's home.

Where Are We?

Because Mark offered no further comment on Jesus's prophecy regarding the destruction of the temple — an event that occurred in AD 70 — we can safely assume that Mark composed the gospel sometime before that tragic event. Also, the gospel has a distinctly Roman feel to it, particularly when compared with the Jewish emphasis of the book of Matthew. Mark chose to leave aside most comments on fulfilled prophecy (compare Matthew 21:1–6 and Mark 11:1–4), and when he felt compelled to use an Aramaic term, he interpreted it (Mark 3:17). This suggests that Mark was in Rome, writing from Peter's recollections sometime before that apostle's death (ca. AD 64–68), possibly composing the gospel between AD 57 and AD 59.

Why Is Mark so Important?

Mark's gospel portrays Jesus as constantly on the move. The forward motion in Mark's writing keeps the knowledgeable reader's mind continually looking ahead to the cross and the resurrection. Thirty-nine times Mark used the word *immediately*, giving a sense that Jesus's time on earth was short and that there was much to accomplish in His few years of ministry.

What's the Big Idea?

While Matthew's gospel portrays Jesus as the King, Mark reveals Him as God's Servant. Jesus's work was always for a larger purpose, a point clearly summarized in Mark 10:45, "For even the Son of Man did not come to be served, but to serve, and to give His life a ransom for many." Mark filled his gospel with the miracles of Jesus, illustrating again and again both the power and the compassion of the Son of God. In these passages, Mark revealed more than Jesus as the good teacher who offered people spiritual renewal; the book also portrays Jesus as the true God and the true man, reaching into the lives of people and effecting physical and circumstantial change.

But Jesus's life as *the* agent of change wasn't without an ultimate purpose. Amid His hands-on ministry, Jesus constantly pointed to the definitive way in which He would serve humanity: His death on the cross and His resurrection from the dead. It is only through faith in these works of Jesus Christ that human beings find eternal redemption for their whole selves. Moreover, Jesus becomes our model for how to live our lives—serving others as He did.

How Do I Apply This?

Three times in three consecutive chapters — 8, 9, and 10 — Mark pictured Jesus informing His disciples of His great sacrifice and ultimate victory. His disciples either rejected the teaching altogether (Mark 8:31–32) or they showed themselves concerned with other matters (9:31–34; 10:32–37). As Jesus prepared to perform the greatest service in the history of the human race, His disciples could only think about themselves — their position or safety.

Do you find it a struggle to get yourself oriented toward sacrificial service, as Jesus's disciples did? The temptations we all wrestle with when faced with an opportunity to serve another person are to pull back within ourselves, to seek our comfort, or to protect our own interests.

The challenge that Jesus presents to us in the book of Mark involves breaking out of those patterns of self-absorption and giving ourselves in service and love to others.

MARK

	Introduction and Preparation	The Servant at Work	The Servant Rejected . . . Then Exalted
	A brief introduction sets Jesus's ministry in motion.	**An unbroken chain of events reveals Jesus helping people in need.**	**A growing discontent among the authorities leads to Jesus's suffering and death.**
	John the Baptizer prepares the way.	Because people are in darkness, He enlightens.	He presses the claim, "Messiah."
	Jesus is tempted in the wilderness.	Because people are sick/afflicted, He heals.	He spends more time alone with His disciples.
		Because people are without hope, He encourages.	He comes into open conflict with His enemies.
		Because people are in bondage to satanic control, He liberates.	He is hated, deserted, tortured, crucified, and buried.
		Because people are sinful, He forgives.	He is raised bodily from the dead!
	CHAPTER 1:1–13	*CHAPTERS 1:14–8:30*	*CHAPTERS 8:31–16:20*
Emphasis		Service to others	Sacrifice for others
Scope		Ministry to the multitudes	Ministry to the Twelve
Sections		Action . . . reaction . . . confrontation	Revelation . . . crucifixion . . . exaltation
Theme	Jesus is the Suffering Servant, who gives His life to save the world.		
Key Verse	10:45		
Christ in Mark	Jesus suffered and died so that salvation would be available to all people (10:45).		

LUKE

—✥—

Who Wrote the Book?

While Luke's name never appears in this gospel, ancient Christian tradition unanimously ascribes the book to him. One ancient prologue written to introduce the gospel describes Luke as a Syrian from Antioch. With this piece of information, we can deduce that Luke was probably not Jewish. Paul also listed him with other Gentiles in his greetings to the Colossians (4:14). The ancient prologue goes on to state that Luke eventually settled in the Greek city of Thebes, where he died at age 84.[1]

Luke's own introduction to his gospel indicates that Luke composed the letter with the purpose of providing a careful rendering of the events of Christ's life in chronological order. As a physician, Luke would have been trained as a careful observer, a quality that would have been invaluable in this project. The result was the first part of a two-volume work written to Theophilus. We know the subsequent volume as Acts.

Where Are We?

Much of the dating of the book of Luke depends on the dating of Acts. Luke's second volume cuts off with Paul imprisoned in Rome, before Paul's death (AD 68) and even before the persecution of Christians broke out under Nero (AD 64). It stands to reason that the book of Luke was completed before Acts. But when?

Acts 21:17 says that Luke accompanied Paul on the apostle's final visit to Jerusalem, a visit that occurred in AD 57–58. Eventually, the Jews had Paul arrested in the temple, a two-year ordeal which ended with Paul's imprisonment in Caesarea. Luke likely used this time apart from

Paul to begin gathering information for writing the gospel from primary sources—those people who had witnessed the ministry, death, and resurrection appearances of Jesus. If Luke took to writing his gospel soon after the information was gathered, then it would have been completed around AD 60, after Paul had been transferred to a Roman prison.

Why Is Luke so Important?

Luke's interest in people is undeniable. Much of the material unique to Luke's gospel involves Jesus's interactions with individuals, many of them on the fringes of "acceptable" society—sinners, women, and children among them. Like Matthew and Mark, Luke recorded the incident of a woman coming to pour perfume on Jesus's feet. But Luke was the only gospel writer to point out the fact known to all present that she was an immoral woman (Luke 7:37). In a similar way, we find in Luke alone the conversation between the robbers crucified alongside Jesus, one of them defending Jesus and receiving the promise of paradise. Luke's portrayal of Jesus reveals in our Lord a man come to minister and show compassion to all people, no matter their station in life.

What's the Big Idea?

Just as Matthew portrays Jesus as the King, and as Mark reveals Him as the Servant, so Luke offers a unique perspective of Jesus as the Son of Man. This phrase, "Son of Man," was Jesus's favorite way to refer to Himself.

Most famous among the people unique to Luke's gospel is the tax collector Zaccheus, a short man who had to climb a tree to see over the crowds as Jesus approached his town. Jesus ended up sharing a meal with Zaccheus at his house, much to the chagrin of the local religious leaders. When Zaccheus expressed his regret over his former way of life and vowed to make restitution, Jesus responded with what became the theme of Luke's gospel: "For the Son of Man has come to seek and to save that which was lost" (Luke 19:10). Luke portrayed Jesus as God's ideal Man, who offers salvation to all humanity—Jew and Gentile alike.

How Do I Apply This?

The richness of Luke's portrayal of Jesus has profound implications for our relationship with God today. Jesus walks through Luke's gospel illustrating His deep and abiding care for people, regardless of what they have done or their status in society.

Do you believe that God loves you no matter what you've done? The fact that the eternal Son of God condescended to lower Himself, take on human flesh, make Himself subject to human limitations, and seek out His people in bodily form shows us clearly how much God cares for us and, in turn, how we are to care for others.

LUKE

The Son of Man

Activity	Preface	Announced and Appearing	Ministering and Serving	Instructing and Submitting	Resurrected and Commissioning
		About 90 percent unique to Luke		About 60 percent unique to Luke	
		"Jesus the Nazarene . . . a prophet . . ."	". . . mighty in deed . . ."	". . . and word in the sight of God and all the people." (24:19)	
	CHAPTER 1:1-4	CHAPTERS 1:5-4:13	CHAPTERS 4:14-9:50	CHAPTERS 9:51-23:56	CHAPTER 24
Activity		Coming	Seeking		Saving
Location		Bethlehem, Nazareth, and Judea	Galilee	Judea and Perea	Jerusalem
Time		About 30 years	1½ years	6 months	8 days / 40 days
Theme		Jesus is the ideal Man, who comes to save all humankind — Jew and Gentile alike.			
Key Verse		19:10			
Christ in Luke		Jesus is the perfect God-man, who comes to offer salvation to all people (19:10).			

JOHN

Who Wrote the Book?

Not surprisingly, the gospel of John never provides the name of its author. Such identifications were not made in any of the other three biblical gospels either. However, two significant factors point to the identification of John as the author. First, the book itself identifies the author as the disciple whom Jesus loved. This description likely pointed to John for three reasons: the author had to be one of the twelve disciples because he was an eyewitness to the events in the gospel (John 21:24); he was probably one of the inner circle of three disciples (James, John, and Peter) because he was among the first Mary told of the resurrection (20:1–10); and this disciple is distinguished from Peter in the book, while James died too soon after the resurrection to be the author.

The second significant evidence for John's authorship is the unanimous testimony of early Christians, among them the second-century Christian Irenaeus, who declared that John was the disciple who laid his head on Jesus—the disciple "whom Jesus loved" (13:23)—and the author of the gospel.

Where Are We?

In Christian tradition, John's gospel has always been referred to as the fourth gospel, meaning it was composed after the other three. Polycarp, a second-century Christian martyr who knew John personally, told Irenaeus that John had written the book during the apostle's time serving the church in Ephesus. These factors suggest that John wrote the book between AD 85 and AD 95.

Why Is John so Important?

John did not include the nativity story in his gospel; instead, he introduced his book by going back even further into history. Invoking the "in the beginning" language of Genesis 1:1, John made a direct link between the nature of God and the nature of the Word, Jesus Christ. The emphasis on the deity of Christ is a striking quality of John's gospel. It also comes through clearly elsewhere in the book, particularly in John 8:58 when Jesus claimed the divine name—"I am"—for Himself, which led an angry mob of Jews to try and kill Him for blasphemy.

What's the Big Idea?

While the other three gospels portray Jesus as the King, the Servant, and the Son of Man, John portrays Jesus as the Son of God. John stated his theme more clearly than any of the other gospel writers. He wrote so that his readers might "believe that Jesus is the Christ, the Son of God," so that they may have life in His name (John 20:31). To accomplish that goal, John presented a riveting and distinctive picture of Jesus Christ, one in complete unity with the portraits in the other three gospels, but one that also adds significantly to the Bible's revelation of Jesus Christ, the God-man.

John used a variety of techniques to communicate to his readers the nature of Jesus. These include his citation of Jesus's seven "I am" statements, in which Jesus spoke of Himself in terms such as "the Light of the world" (8:12), "the resurrection and the life" (11:25), and "the way, and the truth, and the life" (14:6). Much of John's gospel (chapters 2–12) might be called the Book of Signs, as it recounts Jesus's performing of seven different miracles—such as the turning water to wine at Cana and raising Lazarus from the dead at Bethany. These miracles illustrate His identity as the Son of God.

How Do I Apply This?

Jesus's identity as the divine Son of God sets Him apart from any other man who ever lived. He carries with Him the transcendence that comes only with God Himself. Therefore, His work on our behalf makes our salvation sure. Because He is God, His sacrifice on the cross has eternal implications, unlike the limited effect of the animal sacrifices in the Old Testament. Jesus, the God-man, has atoned for our sins. We can place our confidence in Him because of His divine nature.

For readers of John's gospel, the question is a simple, though significant, one: Do you believe that Jesus is Lord? If you believe, you will receive eternal life, claiming the truth that you will one day live in the presence of God in a place with no more pain, no more tears, and no more death.

JOHN

	Deity	God-Man	Ministry	Discourse	Trials and Death	Empty Tomb	Assurance
	"The Word was God." (1:1)	"The Word became flesh." (1:14)	Miraculous signs: Heals invalid at Bethesda (5) Feeds 5,000 (6) Walks on water (6) Heals blind man (9) Raises Lazarus (11)	Private talks: Servanthood (13) Heaven (14) Abiding (15) Promises (16) Prayer (17)	✝	Private talks: Appearances (20)	Private talks: Future (21)
		Miraculous signs: Turns water into wine (2) Heals official's son (4)					
	CHAPTER 1:1–13	CHAPTERS 1:14–4:54	CHAPTERS 5–12	CHAPTERS 13–17	CHAPTERS 18–19	CHAPTER 20	CHAPTER 21
Stage	Prologue	Acceptance	Conflict	Preparation	Crucifixion	Triumph	Epilogue
Audience		Public message	CHANGE		Private message		
Time		Three years			Several days		
Jesus's Seven "I Am" Statements	• "I am the bread of life." (6:35) • "I am the Light of the world." (8:12) • "I am the door." (10:9) • "I am the good shepherd." (10:11)			• "I am the resurrection and the life." (11:25) • "I am the way, and the truth, and the life." (14:6) • "I am the true vine." (15:1)			
Theme	Salvation comes only through Jesus Christ, the Son of God.						
Key Verse	20:31						
Christ in John	Jesus is the Christ, the Son of God, the way, the truth, and the life who alone is the revelation of God and salvation of people (1:1–18; 20:31).						

THE HISTORY OF THE EARLY CHURCH

Acts is unique among the books of the New Testament, for it is the only book to record the history of the early church in the decades just after Christ's ascension. Beginning with just a few disciples, the church, under Peter and Paul, expanded from Jerusalem and beyond — in line with Jesus's final words to His disciples, "You shall be My witnesses both in Jerusalem, and in all Judea and Samaria, and even to the remotest part of the earth" (Acts 1:8).

ACTS

———※———

Who Wrote the Book?

The title of the book of Acts comes from the Greek word *praxis*, a word often used in early Christian literature to describe the great deeds of the apostles or other significant believers. This title accurately reflects the contents of the book, which is a series of vignettes chronicling the lives of key apostles (especially Peter and Paul) in the decades immediately following Christ's ascension into heaven.

Luke's identification as the author of this work was unquestioned throughout ancient times. It shows a clear progression from the gospel according to Luke, picking up just where that book left off. An ancient prologue to Luke's gospel indicates that Luke was first a follower of the apostles and then became close with Paul.[1] This is exactly how the book of Acts unfolds, beginning with Peter and ending with Paul. Luke even began to speak in the first person plural in the latter portion of Acts, as he traveled the Roman Empire alongside Paul (Acts 16:10).

Where Are We?

Acts ends abruptly with Paul imprisoned in Rome, waiting to bring his appeal before Caesar. It is worth noting that in this history of the early Christian church, Luke mentioned neither Paul's death (AD 64–68) nor the persecution of Christians that broke out under Nero (AD 64). More than likely, Luke completed the book before either of these events occurred, sometime between AD 60 and AD 62, while Paul sat in prison, awaiting the resolution of his appeal.

Why Is Acts so Important?

Acts is the only biblical book that chronicles the history of the church immediately after Jesus's ascension. As such, it provides us with a valuable account of how the church was able to grow and spread out from Jerusalem into the rest of the Roman Empire. In only three decades, a small group of frightened believers in Jerusalem transformed into an empire-wide movement of people who had committed their lives to Jesus Christ, ending on a high note with Paul on the verge of taking the gospel to the highest government official in the land—the Emperor of Rome.

What's the Big Idea?

Acts can be neatly divided into two sections, the first dealing primarily with the ministry of Peter in Jerusalem and Samaria (Acts 1–12) and the second following Paul on his missionary journeys throughout the Roman Empire (Acts 13–28). Acts is significant for chronicling the spread of the gospel, not only geographically but also culturally. It records the transition from taking the gospel to an exclusively Jewish audience—with Peter preaching to a small group in the Upper Room—to the gospel going out among the Gentiles, primarily under the ministry of the apostle Paul. The transition is best illustrated by Peter's vision in which he heard a voice telling him, "What God has cleansed, no longer consider unholy" (10:15). This led Peter to then share the gospel with many Gentiles. The lesson? God wants His message of hope and salvation to extend to all people—"in Jerusalem, and in all Judea and Samaria, and even to the remotest part of the earth" (1:8).

How Do I Apply This?

What opportunities for sharing the gospel can you take advantage of in the days to come? This question should ring through your mind as you page through the book of Acts. In virtually every chapter, apostles such as Peter and Paul powerfully present the gospel to individuals and groups of people. The apostles portrayed in Acts shine with evangelistic zeal, showing a striking transition from the often misguided disciples of the Gospels. Clearly the apostles' faith in the death and resurrection of Jesus produced a noticeable change in their hearts through the power of the Holy Spirit.

Too often, our own lives do not reflect that sort of change. We struggle with fears over how others will react to our faith or with breaking out of our own routine long enough to invest in the life of someone else who needs the gospel. Allow Acts to encourage you to walk more closely with God so that you might make Christ's name known with the boldness and the zeal of the apostles.

ACTS

AD 30 ——— AD 60

	The Church Established at "Jerusalem"	The Church Enlarged to "Judea and Samaria"	The Church Expanded to "the Ends of the Earth"
	The church is . . . born tested purified strengthened *CHAPTERS 1–7*	The gospel is . . . spreading multiplying changing lives breaking traditions *CHAPTERS 8–12*	The witness is . . . extended received and rejected changing lives unifying Jews and Gentiles *CHAPTERS 13–28*
Leaders	The apostle Peter	Transition	The apostle Paul
Emphasis	Jewish evangelism	Transition	Gentile evangelism
Time	AD 33 (1:1–2:47)	AD 36 (8:1) — AD 40 (9:32)	AD 46 (13:1) — AD 57 (21:18)
Scope	City evangelism	National evangelism	Cross-cultural evangelism
Theme	In the power of the Holy Spirit, Jesus's followers carry the good news of Christ to the world.		
Key Verse	1:8		
Christ in Acts	Jesus is the glorified, enthroned Savior, who continues His ministry in the world by means of the Holy Spirit working through His disciples until He returns (1:7–9).		

THE PAULINE EPISTLES

The thirteen letters from Romans through Philemon have come to be known as the Pauline Epistles due to their common source, the pen of the apostle Paul. Written primarily to churches with a few addressed to individuals, these letters draw connections between deep theological truths, practical instructions for life, and personal details of the struggles and the joys experienced by the earliest Christians. Most of all, Paul's passion for sharing the gospel shines through clearly in each of these epistles, delivering encouragement to come to faith in Jesus Christ and to live out that faith with consistency and perseverance.

ROMANS

Who Wrote the Book?

Paul had never been to Rome when he wrote the letter to the Romans, though he had clearly expressed his desire to travel there in the near future (Acts 19:21; Romans 1:10–12). The apostle greeted twenty-six different people by name, personalizing a letter from a man who would have been a personal stranger to most of the recipients. No doubt they had heard of Paul and would have been honored by the letter, but Paul always took opportunities to personally connect with his audience so that the message of the gospel might be better received.

Where Are We?

The apostle Paul wrote to the Romans from the Greek city of Corinth in AD 57, just three years after the 16-year-old Nero had ascended to the throne as Emperor of Rome. The political situation in the capital had not yet deteriorated for the Roman Christians, as Nero wouldn't begin his persecution of them until he made them scapegoats after the great Roman fire in AD 64. Therefore, Paul wrote to a church that was experiencing a time of relative peace, but a church that he felt needed a strong dose of basic gospel doctrine.

Writing from Corinth, Paul likely encountered a diverse array of people and practices—from gruff sailors and meticulous tradesmen to wealthy idolaters and enslaved Christians. The prominent Greek city was also a hotbed of sexual immorality and idol worship. So when Paul wrote in Romans about the sinfulness of humanity or the power of God's grace to miraculously and completely change lives, he knew that of which he spoke. It was played out before his eyes every day.

Why Is Romans so Important?

The letter to the Romans stands as the clearest and most systematic presentation of Christian doctrine in all the Scriptures. Paul began by discussing that which is most easily observable in the world—the sinfulness of all humanity. All people have been condemned due to our rebellion against God. However, God in His grace offers us justification by faith in His Son, Jesus. When we are justified by God, we receive redemption, or salvation, because Christ's blood covers our sin. But Paul made it clear that the believer's pursuit of God doesn't stop with salvation; it continues as each of us is sanctified—made holy—as we persist in following Him. Paul's treatment of these issues offers a logical and complete presentation of how a person can be saved from the penalty and power of his or her sin.

What's the Big Idea?

The primary theme running through Paul's letter to the Romans is the revelation of God's righteousness in His plan for salvation, what the Bible calls the gospel:

> For I am not ashamed of the gospel, for it is the power of God for salvation to everyone who believes, to the Jew first and also to the Greek. For in it the righteousness of God is revealed from faith to faith; as it is written, "But the righteous man shall live by faith." (Romans 1:16–17)

Paul showed how human beings lack God's righteousness because of our sin (1–3), receive God's righteousness when God justifies us by faith (4–5), demonstrate God's righteousness by being transformed from rebels to followers (6–8), confirm His righteousness when God saves the Jews (9–11), and apply His righteousness in practical ways throughout our lives (12–16).

How Do I Apply This?

The structure of Romans provides a hint into the importance of the book in our everyday lives. Beginning with eleven chapters of doctrine, the book then transitions into five chapters of practical instruction. This union between doctrine and life illustrates for Christians the absolute importance of both what we believe and how we live out those beliefs. Does your day-to-day life mirror the beliefs you hold, or do you find yourself in a constant battle with hypocrisy? Take heed of the doctrine you find within the pages of Romans, but don't forget to put it into practice as well.

ROMANS

THE GOSPEL

	Saving the Sinner	Concerning Israel	Concerning Christian Conduct
	Depravity of humanity Grace of God Justification by faith Sanctification through the Spirit Security of the saint	Divine sovereignty and human will Past, present, and future of the nation	Social Civil Personal
	CHAPTERS 1:18–8:39	*CHAPTERS 9–11*	*CHAPTERS 12:1–15:13*

Introduction—Personal (1:1–17)

Conclusion—Relational (15:14–16:27)

Emphasis	Doctrinal		National		Practical
Response	Faith		Hope		Love
Doctrine of God	Wrath	Righteousness	Glory		Grace
Doctrine of Humanity	Fallen	Dead	Saved	Struggling	Freed
Doctrine of Sin	Exposed	Conquered	Explained		Forgiven
Scope	Dead in sin	Dead to sin	Peace with God		Love for others
Theme	God's righteousness is given to those who put their faith in Jesus Christ.				
Key Verses	1:16–17				
Christ in Romans	Jesus is the focus of the gospel and the means of salvation by God's grace apart from works (1:1–4, 16–17).				

FIRST CORINTHIANS

Who Wrote the Book?

Paul's authorship of this epistle is widely accepted in the scholarly community, though it was not the first letter Paul wrote to the Corinthian people (see 1 Corinthians 5:9). We know that the Corinthians misunderstood an earlier letter from Paul (5:10–11), though that letter has not survived. Therefore, it is Paul's second letter to the Corinthians that we know as 1 Corinthians—the first letter to the Corinthians that God inspired.

Four years prior to writing the letter we know as 1 Corinthians, the apostle had spent eighteen months in Corinth, so he was intimately familiar with the church and many of its congregants. The recipients of the letter must have understood the letter's significance, not only to their own circumstances but for the church worldwide. In AD 95, Clement, the bishop of Rome, wrote a letter of his own to the Corinthians in which he invoked the authority of Paul's instruction in 1 Corinthians. Only a few decades after its origin, this letter to the Corinthians had traveled outside of Corinth and was considered authoritative beyond its initial Corinthian context.

Where Are We?

Paul had been in Ephesus for more than two years on his third missionary journey when he received a disturbing report of quarreling within the Corinthian church, a report he received from people associated with one of its members, Chloe (1 Corinthians 1:11). The church he had founded so recently (Acts 18:1–17) had already developed deep divisions, a situation that required immediate action. Paul penned his letter in AD 55, just as he was planning to leave Ephesus for Macedonia (1 Corinthians 16:5–8).

Why Is First Corinthians so Important?

First Corinthians contains a frank discussion of the church and the issues that impacted real people in the first century. The Corinthian church was corroded with sin on a variety of fronts, so Paul provided an important model for how the church should handle the problem of sin in its midst. Rather than turn a blind eye toward relational division and all kinds of immorality, he addressed the problems head on. In his bold call to purity within the Corinthian church, Paul made it clear that he was willing to risk the good opinion of some in order to help cleanse the sin that tainted the church.

What's the Big Idea?

First Corinthians addresses reports that Paul received from Chloe's household, as well as a letter he received from the church itself (1 Corinthians 7:1). In this letter to the church at Corinth, Paul covered a number of different issues related to both life and doctrine: divisions and quarrels, sexual immorality, lawsuits among believers, marriage and singleness, freedom in Christ, order in worship, the significance of the Lord's Supper, and the right use of spiritual gifts; he also included a profound teaching on the resurrection.

The line of thought that joins these topics together was Paul's emphasis on Christian conduct in the local church. The apostle expected that Christian people would live according to Christian ideals, or as he told them, "You have been bought with a price: therefore glorify God in your body" (6:20).

How Do I Apply This?

Corinth was a large, international metropolis, filled with people from different backgrounds. Idol worship to gods such as Aphrodite was particularly prominent in the city, though Corinth contained numerous temptations far beyond her temples. In this sense, Corinth was very much like a modern urban area, containing unending opportunities to engage in sinful behavior without any apparent consequences.

Such a community clearly had a negative influence on the Corinthian church. But notice that Paul's instruction to the believers was not to retreat from their city. This was not Paul's vision for the church then or now. Instead, he directed us to live out our commitment to Christ ever more faithfully in the midst of nonbelievers. Paul expected that we Christians would shine our light into the dark places of their world by worshiping in a unified community that was accountable to one another. He expected that we would settle our problems internally, that we would encourage one another in the pursuit of purity, and that we would strive together by holding tightly to the hope of our bodily resurrection to come.

What can you do within your local church to make this kind of community more of a reality?

FIRST CORINTHIANS

	Rebuke for Sinful Conditions		Reply to Specific Questions
	Divisions in the Church	**Disorders in the Church**	**Difficulties in the Church**
	Exposition (1:10–17)	Moral disorder (5:1–13)	Domestic difficulty—marriage and divorce (7:1–40)
	Explanation (1:18–4:5)	Legal disorder (6:1–11)	Social difficulty—liberty and license (8:1–11:1)
	Exhortation (4:6–21)	Carnal disorder (6:12–20)	Ecclesiastical difficulty—women and worship (11:2–34)
			Practical difficulty—gifts and body (12:1–14:40)
			Doctrinal difficulty—death and resurrection (15:1–58)
			Financial difficulty—gifts and body (16:1–9)
	CHAPTERS 1:10–4:21	*CHAPTERS 5–6*	*CHAPTERS 7:1–16:9*

Introduction (1:1–9)   Conclusion (16:10–24)

Key	"I exhort you." (1:10)	"Now concerning the thing about which you wrote." (7:1)
Need	Unity among the Corinthian Christians	Clarity regarding six areas of concern
Theme	Christian conduct in the local church	
Key Verses	6:9–11; 13:1–38	
Christ in 1 Corinthians	Jesus is the source of unity among believers who are baptized into the body of Christ and the basis of their ultimate resurrection and glorification (12:12–13; 15:1–58).	

34

SECOND CORINTHIANS

—⁂—

Who Wrote the Book?

Paul wrote 2 Corinthians at a vulnerable time in his life. He had learned that the church at Corinth was struggling, and he sought to take action to preserve the unity of that local body of believers. The letter is riddled with personal comments as Paul revealed details about the persecution he had suffered for the sake of Christ as well as about a mysterious thorn in the flesh that kept him reliant on God.

Where Are We?

After sending Timothy off from Ephesus to deliver the letter of 1 Corinthians, Paul, in his concern for the church, made a quick visit of his own to Corinth. Afterward, Paul returned to his work in Ephesus, where he wrote a sorrowful letter to the Corinthians that has not been preserved (see 2 Corinthians 2:1–11; 7:8). Paul then departed for Macedonia. Once there, he received a good report from Titus regarding the Corinthians (7:13), which led Paul to write a fourth letter to them, titled "2 Corinthians" in the Bible. (See the previous chapter in this handbook to read about Paul's first two letters to the Corinthians.) The apostle composed this letter near the end of AD 56, possibly in the city of Philippi.

Why Is Second Corinthians so Important?

This letter offers a great deal of personal insight into Paul's life that is not present in any other New Testament book. However, in chapters 8 and 9, his letter also clearly reveals God's plan for His people to give to others. Paul first focused on the generous example of the Macedonian churches, largely Gentile, who gave to their Jewish Christian brothers and sisters in Jerusalem. Then he exhorted the Corinthian believers to make donations of their own to the work in Jerusalem. Several realities about Christian giving become clear in these two chapters: Christians give generously according to, and at times beyond, their financial abilities; Christians give their money across racial and national lines; Christians who make commitments to give should follow through with those promises; and Christians should give cheerfully, rather than under compulsion.

What's the Big Idea?

The church at Corinth had recently been struggling with divisions and quarrels. But for a majority of the believers, the problem had been solved by the time Paul wrote 2 Corinthians. Many had repented of their sinful ways and had come back into unity with one another and with the leadership of Paul.

However, Paul still felt the need to articulate a defense of his apostleship and his message. Some in the church had apparently taken his meekness among them to be a sign of moral weakness or lack of authority (2 Corinthians 10:1–2). These accusations led Paul to defend himself by arguing that he was on the same level of importance as the other apostles, that he had deep knowledge of the Christian faith, that he had suffered profound physical punishment in the name of Christ, and that he had received visions and revelations from God (11:1–12:13).

How Do I Apply This?

Just as Paul wrote to the Corinthians in the wake of their repentance from divisions and quarrels, the message for today is clear: living in unity requires us to humbly forgive one another and to follow our leaders. Second Corinthians reminds us that even as Christians, we hurt each other and need to forgive those who wrong us (2 Corinthians 2:7). That Paul was willing to exhort the Corinthian believers to forgive those who had fallen away and repented, even as he defended his own apostleship against a vocal opposition, illustrates the apostle's commitment to this way of life among God's people.

In what ways do you struggle to forgive others and/or to follow your godly leaders? An overinflated sense of ourselves often leads us to strike out on our own or hold on to our frustration and anger regarding the choices of others. However, just as Paul reminded us of Jesus's ministry of reconciliation (5:17–19), we must seek to reconcile relationships in which disunity reigns. Look out for the pitfall of disunity with leaders and other believers in your own life while striving to live among all people in humility.

SECOND CORINTHIANS

Conclusion — Farewell (13:11–14)

	Crucial Concerns	Grace Giving	Apostolic Authority
	Suffering and God's comfort	Example of Macedonians	Reply to critics
	New covenant ministry	Command to Corinthians	Justification of ministry
	Persevering in godliness		False teachers
			Visions, revelations, credentials, warnings
			God's power perfected in weakness
	CHAPTERS 1:3–7:16	*CHAPTERS 8–9*	*CHAPTERS 10:1–13:10*
Scope	Past	Present	Future
Issue	Misunderstandings, concerns, explanations	Financial project	Vindication of Paul's ministry
Tone	Forgiving, grateful, bold	Confident	Defensive and strong
Theme	Paul's defense of his apostleship and message		
Key Verses	4:5	9:7	10:8
Christ in 2 Corinthians	Jesus is the One who comforts us in our suffering, reconciles us to God, and gives strength in our weaknesses (1:5; 5:17–21; 12:9).		

GALATIANS

Who Wrote the Book?

Galatians has always been among those Pauline epistles least challenged on the issue of authorship. Paul wrote to the churches in southern Galatia after having a hand in starting them on his first missionary journey to Asia Minor. Paul's close relationship to these churches helps to explain the extremely strong tone he took with them from the very beginning of the letter. Galatians exhibits Paul at his angriest, as he risked the good favor of the converts in those churches to make sure they were on the path of truth and not led off into deception. In fact, to emphasize the seriousness of his purpose, he took the pen from his scribe and wrote the end of the letter himself in large letters (Galatians 6:11).

Where Are We?

Upon arriving back in Antioch from his first missionary journey after eighteen months on the road, Paul received a report that the churches he had started in Galatia had fallen into hard times—specifically, they had fallen into error. A group of Judaizers—those who sought to make living under the Mosaic Law a requirement of the Christian faith—had gained an influence in the Galatian churches. Paul wrote the book a few months before his attendance at the Jerusalem Council in AD 49, a meeting where the apostles would take up this very topic (Acts 15:1–30).

Why Is Galatians so Important?

In advance of the Jerusalem Council, Paul's letter speaks wisdom and clarity into the first real controversy that plagued the church in its early years—the relationship between Christian Jews and Christian Gentiles.

Paul's aggressive tone shows just how important it was to him that the people embrace unity in Christ, no matter their racial distinctions. For him, this was no minor issue, as he went so far as to call the Galatians deserters of Christ, people turning from the truth toward a gospel contrary to the one they had received from Paul (Galatians 1:6–9).

What's the Big Idea?

When the Galatians fell away so quickly from the gospel of grace Paul had preached to them, they also made clear their disloyalty to Paul's authority as an apostle. Therefore, Paul began the letter to the Galatians by spending two chapters defending that very issue. Only in chapter 3 did he begin to get to the heart of their error; namely, that these Galatians sought to be justified by the Mosaic Law. In contrast, Paul presented his argument that justification comes to people by faith in Jesus Christ, not by their works under the Law.

Part of the problem that confronted the Galatians came in one of the arguments made by the Judaizers. These false teachers suggested that to live by grace and in freedom meant to live a lawless and therefore degenerate life. And so in the final chapters of the letter, Paul made clear that justification—an act of grace through faith—need not result in a sinful lifestyle. Because Christians have been freed from bondage to the sinful nature, we now have the path of holiness open to us.

How Do I Apply This?

Unfortunately, the false teaching brought to the Galatian churches by the Judaizers has been extremely difficult to root out even today. We must walk a fine line—on one hand, we do not want to fall into the legalism that the Galatians struggled with, but on the other, we cannot just live as if anything goes. The Christian's commitment to Christ is based on the free gift of grace through faith, but as Paul articulated at the end of Galatians, it also results in a life of walking by the Spirit.

Is the fruit of the Spirit evident in your life, or do you find yourself living according to the flesh or "the compulsions of selfishness" (Galatians 5:16–26 MSG)? Too often we lose ourselves at the extremes, ending in a legalistic attempt to earn our salvation or a devil-may-care attitude about our sin.

Use Paul's words in Galatians as an encouragement to pursue a life of holiness, not in your own strength but in the knowledge of God's empowering grace in your life.

GALATIANS

	Personal Words from Paul	Doctrinal Teaching	Practical Exhortations
	Defense of the True Gospel	**Freedom from Legalism**	**Freedom to Love and to Serve**
	For I would have you know, brethren, that the gospel which was preached by me is not according to man. For I neither received it from man, nor was I taught it, but I received it through a revelation of Jesus Christ. (1:11–12)	Therefore the Law has become our tutor to lead us to Christ, so that we may be justified by faith. But now that faith has come, we are no longer under a tutor. (3:24–25)	For you were called to freedom, brethren; only do not turn your freedom into an opportunity for the flesh, but through love serve one another. (5:13)
	CHAPTERS 1–2	*CHAPTERS 3–4*	*CHAPTERS 5–6*
Style	Vigorous, blunt, direct, and brief		
Theme	Justification comes by faith in Christ Jesus, not by works of the Law.		
Key Verse	2:16		
Christ in Galatians	Jesus is the source and power of the believer's new life and the heir of the promises to Abraham's seed (2:20; 3:1–16).		

EPHESIANS

Who Wrote the Book?

For a brief time at the end of his second missionary journey, and then for more than two years on his third missionary journey, Paul ministered to the church at Ephesus (Acts 18:18–21; 19:1–41). During his time in this city that housed the famous temple to the Greek goddess Artemis, Paul saw many converted to faith in Jesus Christ and many others who opposed his preaching in the synagogues and homes. One prominent silversmith, Demetrius, who made implements for the worship of Artemis, found his business suffering greatly because people were converting to Christianity. The ensuing near-riot led Paul to leave the city, but only after the apostle had done much to stabilize and grow the Christian community there.

Where Are We?

Paul wrote the letter to the Ephesians sometime in AD 60–61, around the same time he wrote Colossians and Philemon, as he sent all three letters by the hand of Tychicus, accompanied by Onesimus (Ephesians 6:21; Colossians 4:7–9; Philemon 1:10–12). It was during this time that Paul sat in Rome undergoing his first Roman imprisonment (Ephesians 3:1; 4:1), making Ephesians one of the four epistles commonly known as the Prison Epistles. The others are Philippians, Colossians, and Philemon.

Why Is Ephesians so Important?

Second Corinthians and Galatians abound with personal touches from Paul, either about his own life or that of the recipients. Ephesians, on the other hand, stands at the opposite end of the spectrum as one of

Paul's most formal letters. While Galatians offers instructions particularly important for those churches overrun with legalism, Ephesians deals with topics at the very core of what it means to be a Christian—both in faith and in practice—regardless of any particular problem in the community.

What's the Big Idea?

Paul divided his letter to the Ephesians into two clear segments; applying the truths of the first makes possible the actions and lifestyle of the second. Paul spent the first three chapters of the letter discussing God's creation of a holy community by His gift of grace in the death and resurrection of Jesus Christ. The members of this community have been chosen by God through the work of Christ, adopted as sons and daughters of God, and brought near to the Father through faith in His Son. All people with this faith—Jews and Gentiles alike—were dead in their transgressions and sins but have been made alive because of the person and work of Jesus Christ.

While Paul was not responding to a particular theological or moral problem, he wanted to protect against future problems by encouraging the Ephesians to mature in their faith. So after laying out profound theological truths in the first half of the book, Paul made his purpose clear: he expected that this community of faith would walk in accordance with its heavenly calling (Ephesians 4:1). As a result of the theological realities Christians accept by their faith in God, several practices should follow in their relationships within the church, in the home, and in the world.

How Do I Apply This?

The book of Ephesians hits on a wide range of moral and ethical behaviors, designed to ensure believers are living up to our heavenly calling. As we continue in our faith from day to day, month to month, and year to year, the temptation to get comfortable will always exist. However, Paul presented the gift of God in Christ and the benefits we receive so clearly that we cannot help but ask ourselves if our lives reflect that reality as they should.

How have you grown in your Christian life since you came to faith in Jesus Christ? The latter half of Ephesians makes clear that spiritual growth occurs primarily in community with others, iron sharpening iron (Proverbs 27:17). Your Christian "walk" (in other words, your daily life) is to be characterized by unity, holiness, love, wisdom, and perseverance in spiritual warfare.

Maturity yields benefits in believers' moral lives, but it extends far beyond that as well. Increased maturity benefits the community at large, leading us as Christians to present a more consistent witness to the working of God in our lives as well as protecting us from the harmful divisions and quarrels that have plagued so many communities throughout history.

EPHESIANS

	Our Position in Christ	Our Practice on Earth
	Section 1: What God has done for us (1) Emphasis: sovereignty	Section 1: Our new unity (4:1–16)
	Section 2: What Christ has done in us (2:1–10) Emphasis: grace	Section 2: Our new walk (4:17–6:9)
	Section 3: What Christ has done between us (2:11–3:21) Emphasis: reconciliation	Section 3: Our new strength (6:10–20)
	CHAPTERS *1–3*	*CHAPTERS* *4–6*
Emphasis	Doctrinal: vertical relationship with God	Practical: horizontal relationship with others
Core Phrase	"He chose us in Him." (1:4)	"Walk in a manner worthy of the calling." (4:1)
Subjects	Declarations of heavenly truths (God's accomplishments)	Exhortations for earthly living (Christians' assignments)
Prayers	Paul's prayer for Ephesians (1:15–23)	Paul's prayer for the whole church (3:14–21)	Christians' prayers for one another (6:18–20)
Theme	The holy community God is creating and how it is to live out its calling	
Key Verses	1:9–10; 4:1–3	
Christ in Ephesians	Jesus is the source of spiritual blessing, the Cornerstone of the church, and the goal of spiritual maturity (1:3; 2:20; 4:11–16).	

PHILIPPIANS

Who Wrote the Book?

Paul ministered at Philippi during his second missionary journey, spending about three months in the city. The ministry at Philippi marked Paul's entrance into Macedonia, which came about as a result of a vision he had in the city of Troas, just across the northeastern corner of the Aegean Sea from the port city of Neapolis and its close neighbor Philippi (Acts 16:8–12).

During this first stay in Philippi—he later briefly visited the city on his third missionary journey (20:6)—Paul brought to faith in Christ people who would form the core of the burgeoning congregation in the city. Among them were Lydia, a businesswoman who opened her home to Paul and his coworkers (16:13–15), and the Philippian jailer, who was converted under Paul's ministry after an earthquake miraculously broke open the prison (16:22–34).

Where Are We?

Of the four Prison Epistles, Paul likely wrote Philippians last, near the end of his Roman imprisonment in AD 61 or 62. Paul sent the other three Prison Epistles—Ephesians, Colossians, and Philemon—by the hand of Tychicus, as their destinations were near one another. However, the letter to the Philippians was to be delivered by Epaphroditus, who had come to Paul in Rome with financial help from the church at Philippi (Philippians 2:25; 4:18). But during his time in Rome, Epaphroditus took ill, which delayed his return home and, therefore, the delivery of the letter (2:26–27).

Why Is Philippians so Important?

The apostle Paul did not write Philippians in response to a crisis, as he did with Galatians and Colossians. Instead, he wrote to express his appreciation and affection for the Philippian believers. More than any other church, the believers in Philippi offered Paul material support for his ministry (2 Corinthians 8:11; Philippians 4:15–18). Paul's affection for these people is clear throughout the letter as he encouraged them to live out their faith in joy and unity (1:3–5, 25–26; 4:1).

What's the Big Idea?

Philippians brims over with often quoted passages: "He who began a good work in you will perfect it until the day of Christ Jesus" (Philippians 1:6), "To live is Christ and to die is gain" (1:21), and "I can do all things through Him who strengthens me" (4:13) are just a few. But the portrait of Jesus Christ as a humble servant serves as the core of Paul's teaching in this letter (2:5–11).

Paul's joy at the mere thought of the Philippian church is undeniable in the letter, and it's that same joy that he wanted the recipients to possess as well. To lead the Philippians to this truth, Paul took them directly to Jesus, teaching them that a community of believers living in harmony with one another comes only through mutual humility modeled after the Savior. Paul wrote that he poured out his life as an offering for the sake of Christ, leading Paul to find great joy and contentment in Christ's service. His letter to the Philippians showed them that by centering their lives on Christ, they, too, might live in true joy.

How Do I Apply This?

Though we all have much to be thankful for, the pace and the pressure of life often squeeze the joy from us. Our shoulders slumped and our heads bowed, we find some days—or months—very difficult to get through. Desperate, we often search for joy in all kinds of ways—acquiring possessions, visiting places, or seeing people. But none of these can provide lasting joy. Where do you find joy in the midst of a trying circumstance?

Paul knew, as did the Philippians, that true joy comes only through humble faith in the saving work of Jesus Christ, joining ourselves in harmony with His followers, and serving others in the name of Christ. This was the life experienced by the Philippian believers, and it is a life available to us today.

Allow the joy you find in Christ to keep you from useless quarrels and divisions and to instead guide you into harmonious relationships with God's people.

PHILIPPIANS

	Joy in Living for Christ	Joy in Serving Christ in Unity	Joy in Knowing Christ	Joy in Resting in Christ
	Even when we don't get what we want In spite of circumstances Even with conflicts	Starts with right attitude Maintained through right theology Encouraged by right models	A warning A testimony A goal A command	Unity Peace Final predictions
	CHAPTER 1	*CHAPTER 2*	*CHAPTER 3*	*CHAPTER 4*
Christ	. . . my Life	. . . my Model	. . . my Goal	. . . my Contentment
Spirit	His provision (1:19)	His fellowship (2:1)	His worship (3:3)	His peace (4:7)
Positive Reaction	To difficulty: "Now I want you to know, brethren, that my circumstances have turned out for the greater progress of the gospel." (1:12)	To others: "Do all things without grumbling or disputing." (2:14)	To the past:"Forgetting what lies behind and reaching forward to what lies ahead, I press on toward the goal for the prize." (3:13–14)	To the "unchangeables": "Not that I speak from want, for I have learned to be content in whatever circumstances I am." (4:11)
Tone	Warm, encouraging, affirming			
Key Words	"Rejoice," "Christ," "Mind," "Act"			
Uniqueness	No major problem passages. "Joy" is found in each chapter. Not one quotation from the Old Testament. Christ mentioned over forty times. Most positive of all Paul's letters, yet written while he was chained to a Roman guard.			
Theme	By centering our lives around Christ, we can experience true joy.			
Key Verse	1:21			
Christ in Philippians	Jesus is the Son of God from heaven, who humbled Himself by becoming human, who suffered for us, and who was exalted to heaven (2:5–11).			

COLOSSIANS

—⚜—

Who Wrote the Book?

Before Paul wrote this letter to the Christians in Colossae, he had never been to their city (Colossians 2:1). This helps explain the personal greetings he included at the end of the letter, a practice he usually reserved for letters to churches he had not visited (for example, Romans). Paul sought to develop personal connections with the people he hoped to teach and serve, rather than just going around from city to city asserting his apostolic authority. The more personal tone at the close of this letter would have been especially significant in creating a connection with the Colossian believers, given the fact that part of Paul's reason for writing involved calling out the heretical teachers who had infiltrated the Colossian church.

Where Are We?

In AD 60–61, during his first imprisonment in Rome, Paul penned this letter to the Colossian church after he had received a report that they were struggling with a christological heresy. The report came from Epaphras, likely the leader of the church at Colossae and a convert of Paul's from his more than two-year ministry in Ephesus. Epaphras had come to Rome in part to serve Paul during his imprisonment (Philemon 1:23) but also to confide in him regarding the dangerous teachings the Colossians were hearing. So Paul sent this letter, along with the letters to Philemon and to the Ephesians, with Tychicus, accompanied by Onesimus (Colossians 4:7; Philemon 1:10–12). Tychicus was a coworker of Paul who would have been able to help the Colossian believers understand and apply the apostle's teachings in the letter.

Why Is Colossians so Important?

The church at Colossae was under attack from false teachers who were denigrating the deity of Jesus; they were teaching that He was not actually God. Though Paul had never been to the church itself, he addressed these issues head-on. The nature of Jesus Christ as Creator and Redeemer was nonnegotiable, so Paul wrote to them that he might bring his wisdom to bear on this difficult and trying situation. It was critical to him that this church know God in His greatness and glory, rather than in the deficient view given them by the false teachers (Colossians 1:25; 2:1–2).

What's the Big Idea?

In this book, the apostle Paul described Jesus with some of the loftiest language in all the New Testament, focusing on Christ's preeminence and sufficiency in all things. Paul presented Christ as the center of the universe, not only as the active Creator but also as the recipient of creation—in His taking on of human flesh. Christ was and is the visible image of the invisible God, containing within Himself the fullness of Deity (Colossians 2:9). Because of His divine nature, Jesus is sovereign, above all things with an authority given Him by the Father. As such, Jesus is also Head over the church. He has reconciled all things to Himself through His death on the cross, making believers alive to God and setting them on the path to right living. This proper view of Christ served as the antidote for the Colossian heresy as well as a building block for Christian life and doctrine both then and now.

How Do I Apply This?

Your view of Jesus Christ will impact every area of your life. Many today want only practical instruction and helps for living, eschewing "esoteric" topics such as doctrine and theology because they seem to be out of touch with their day-to-day reality. Paul's view was different. He saw that the christological problems in the Colossian church had practical importance as well. Believers have died with Christ; therefore, we need to die to our sins. We have also been raised with Christ; therefore, we must live well in Him and put on qualities that are motivated by Christian love. And because He is Lord over all, the life of the Christian is a life of submission to Jesus. Are you following after Jesus as you should? Our faith in Jesus Christ should transform the relationships we have in every area of our lives—in our homes, our churches, and our world.

COLOSSIANS

Subject	Christ Is Our Lord		. . . Our Life	. . . Our Love
	Lord of creation	Lord of our walk	Our mind	Love for "outsiders"
	Lord of the church	Lord of our salvation	Our body	Love for believers
	Lord of ministry	Lord of our growth	Our attitude	
			Our actions	
	CHAPTER 1	CHAPTER 2	CHAPTER 3	CHAPTER 4
Subject	Instruction	Warnings	Exhortations	Reminders
Christ	His person and work		His peace and presence	
Emphasis	Doctrinal and corrective		Practical and reassuring	
Theme	Christ is our supreme Lord and sufficient Savior.			
Key Verses	2:9–10			
Christ in Colossians	Jesus is the supreme Lord of the church and the world, the all-sufficient Savior in whom the fullness of Deity dwells (1:13–20; 2:9).			

FIRST THESSALONIANS

—⧖—

Who Wrote the Book?

After Paul started the church in Thessalonica, he wrote this first letter to the believers there within just a few months of leaving. In Acts, Luke recorded that Paul preached for three Sabbath days to the Jews in the local synagogue (Acts 17:2). However, most scholars believe Paul spent about three months, rather than three weeks, with the Thessalonians because he would have had to have been there long enough to receive more than one offering from the Philippian church (Philippians 4:15–16).

Paul's ministry in Thessalonica obviously touched not only Jews but Gentiles as well. Many Gentiles in the church had come out of idolatry, which was not a particular problem among the Jews of that time (1 Thessalonians 1:9).

Where Are We?

Paul wrote his first letter to the Thessalonian church from the city of Corinth around AD 51, just a few months after having preached in Thessalonica on his second missionary journey. Upon leaving Thessalonica under duress, Paul, Silas, and Timothy traveled to Athens by way of Berea. But after a short time in Athens, Paul felt the need to receive a report from the newborn church in Thessalonica, so he sent Timothy back to serve and minister to the new believers there. Paul wanted to check on the state of the Thessalonians' faith, for fear that false teachers might have infiltrated their number. However, Timothy soon returned with a good report, prompting Paul to pen 1 Thessalonians as a letter of encouragement to the new believers.

Why Is First Thessalonians so Important?

Everyone would like to have some insight into what their future holds. How much more so when it comes to the end of the whole world? First Thessalonians provides Christians with the clearest biblical passage on the coming rapture of believers, an event that will inaugurate the seven-year tribulation. At the rapture, Christ will return for His people. The dead in Christ shall rise first, while those still living will follow close behind. All believers will meet Jesus in the air to begin an eternity spent with the Lord (1 Thessalonians 4:16–18).

What's the Big Idea?

Impressed by the faithfulness of the Thessalonians in the face of persecution, Paul wrote to encourage the Christians in that community with the goal that they would continue to grow in godliness. Paul knew that the people had been exposed to errant teaching from those in opposition to the way of Jesus Christ and the grace of God. And Paul also understood that unless the young church continued to mature in its faith, the danger would only increase over time.

With that in mind, Paul taught the people that any spiritual growth would ultimately be motivated by their hope in the ultimate return of Jesus Christ. Paul was never interested in simply telling people to pull themselves up by their bootstraps, for he knew that what ultimately inspired change was a life of consistently walking in the power of God's Spirit. And so to a group of young Christians with questions and uncertainties, Paul offered the hope of Christ's return, providing both comfort in the midst of questions and motivation to godly living.

How Do I Apply This?

Do you ever feel as though your Christian faith has grown stale, that you are withering on the vine when you would rather be flourishing in His service? Paul's first letter to the Thessalonians is the perfect remedy for such a feeling. Its focus on Christ's return provides water for the thirsty soul today, encouraging growth in maturity by providing hope in the midst of suffering or uncertainty.

Paul's specific, practical instruction for this process of sanctification can be applied directly to our current circumstances. By clinging to our hope in Christ, we may see several clear results in our lives: avoiding sexual immorality, refusing to defraud others, appreciating those Christians who serve on your behalf, refusing to repay evil for evil, rejoicing always, praying without ceasing, and giving thanks in all things — to name a few (1 Thessalonians 4:3–7; 5:12–23). This list, of course, is not exhaustive, but the first letter to the Thessalonians makes clear that every Christian should expect to grow in holiness over the course of his or her life.

FIRST THESSALONIANS

	The Pastor's Heart			The Pastor's Burden	
	Thanksgiving / Remembering / Affirming / Reporting	The pastor among the flock / The flock's response to the pastor	Personal concern / Comfort and relief	Sexual purity / Prophetic urgency	Stay alert! / Encourage one another! / Live in peace!
	CHAPTER 1	CHAPTER 2	CHAPTER 3	CHAPTER 4	CHAPTER 5
Perspective		Looking back		Looking ahead	
Subject	The church itself	The apostle himself	The report	The concern	The balance
Especially Appropriate for . . .	new converts	young pastors	suffering Christians	tempted and uninformed Christians	"sleepy" Christians
Theme	The hope of Christ's return comforts us and motivates us to godly living.				
Key Verses	1:8–10; 4:1, 13–18				
Christ in 1 Thessalonians	Jesus is our source of hope and comfort, the One who rescues believers from the coming wrath (1:10; 4:13–5:11).				

SECOND THESSALONIANS

—✠—

Who Wrote the Book?

Just because Paul visited a city, preached the gospel for weeks or even months, and founded a church by guiding converts to the faith, this did not protect the new church from scheming heretics. In fact, the immaturity of any new church presented a perfect target for those who meant to mislead and distort the truth. Paul, worried about his friends and their troubles with false teachers, wrote this second letter to the believers at Thessalonica in the hope of encouraging their young but burgeoning faith.

Where Are We?

Paul wrote 2 Thessalonians from Corinth in AD 51 within months of writing the first letter. Since the subject matter of the second letter has a number of thematic similarities to the first, Paul probably had received a second report from the city detailing continuing questions or problems regarding the end times. Several of Paul's references indicate that some in Thessalonica were deliberately misleading these new believers, even to the point of false teachers forging letters to make them look as if they had come from Paul (2 Thessalonians 2:2). The apostle, therefore, took extra care in this letter to make sure the Thessalonians understood not only his views on the end times but also what his handwriting looked like, so they would be able to identify letters as authentically his (3:17).

Why Is Second Thessalonians so Important?

Second Thessalonians distinguishes itself by the detailed teaching it presents on the end times. False teachers had been presenting fake letters as if from Paul and telling the Thessalonian believers that the day of the Lord had already come. This would have been especially troubling to them because Paul had encouraged them in his previous letter that they would be raptured before the day of wrath came upon the earth.

So Paul explained to them that this future time of tribulation had not yet come because a certain "man of lawlessness" had not yet been revealed (2 Thessalonians 2:3). Comparisons with other passages in Daniel, Matthew, and Revelation reveal this man to be none other than the Antichrist. But Paul encouraged the Thessalonians not to worry, because the Antichrist would not come until a mysterious restrainer—the Thessalonians apparently knew his identity—was removed from earth (2:6–7). The identity of this restrainer has been heavily debated, though due to the nature of the work the restrainer does, He is likely the Spirit of God working redemptively through the church. When the believers leave the earth in the rapture, all who remain will experience the wrath of the tribulation.

What's the Big Idea?

The apostle Paul, in concern for the Thessalonian believers who were trying to stand firm in their faith under pressure from false teachers, taught the Thessalonians in this letter that their hope in Christ's future return should serve as an encouragement to them in their suffering, motivating them to live responsibly for Him. Paul always connected his teaching on Jesus with the practical growth he expected to see as a result of such a deeply held faith.

How Do I Apply This?

Discipline and self-control are two qualities that quickly slip away in a society so focused on the material that its people forget the spiritual realities that should dictate their lives. Fat with financial and material success, many people today have descended into an unruly and lazy existence that possesses little care for others, especially of the kind that might conflict with our personal, fleshly desires. How does your daily life come into conflict with God's desire for you to live well and serve others?

Paul knew that hope in Christ would encourage perseverance in godly living. And hope is exactly what we lack today, one of the great roots of this gradual slip into increased self-centeredness. As you read the words of 2 Thessalonians, allow them to rekindle your hope and fan into flame your desire to live in God-honoring, industrious ways.

SECOND THESSALONIANS

	Affirmation amidst Affliction	Explanation of Prophecy	Clarification regarding Response
	"We ought always to give thanks to God for you." (1:3)	"Let no one in any way deceive you." (2:3)	"We command you." (3:6)
	"We . . . speak proudly of you . . . for your perseverance and faith." (1:4)	Secret power of lawlessness	"If anyone does not obey" (3:14)
		Restraint removed	"May the Lord of peace Himself continually grant you peace." (3:16)
	"We pray for you always." (1:11)	Man of lawlessness	
		"So then . . . stand firm." (2:15)	
	CHAPTER 1	*CHAPTER 2*	*CHAPTER 3*
Question	Why are we suffering?	What will occur?	How do I respond?
Contrasts	Peace amidst pain	Lawlessness versus restraint	Work while waiting
Statement	The Lord knows!	The "day of the Lord" has not yet come!	"Do not grow weary of doing good." (3:13)
Emphasis	Commendation	Correction	Clarification
Theme	The hope of Christ's return encourages us in our suffering and motivates us to live responsibly for Him.		
Key Verses	1:11–12; 2:13–15		
Christ in 2 Thessalonians	Jesus is the coming Judge who will reward the righteous and destroy the wicked, including the coming man of lawlessness in the end times (1:6–2:12).		

FIRST TIMOTHY

—— ✥ ——

Who Wrote the Book?

The first of Paul's final series of letters—which along with 2 Timothy and Titus are called the Pastoral Epistles—1 Timothy offers practical and pastoral advice from the aging apostle Paul to a young pastor named Timothy working in the church at Ephesus. More than a decade prior to writing this letter, Paul had first met Timothy in the city of Lystra—in Asia Minor—where Timothy was known and respected by the Christians (Acts 16:1–4). Upon recognizing Timothy's impressive qualities, Paul recruited the young man to travel with him as he continued his second missionary journey. The presence of Timothy would have met an important need for Paul, their friendship coming on the heels of Paul's split with his close friend and partner in missions, Barnabas (15:36–41).

Where Are We?

The Bible's silence on the ultimate fate of Paul has engendered a great deal of debate in modern times. The book of Acts ends with Paul sitting in a Roman prison awaiting his hearing before the Roman emperor, a privilege of appeal that all Roman citizens possessed. However, the writing of the Pastoral Epistles clearly dates to a time after the events of Acts. So where was Paul when he wrote 1 Timothy? Paul had expected the Romans to release him from prison, something that likely happened near the end of AD 62 (Philippians 2:24). His release allowed him the opportunity to travel to Ephesus and eventually place Timothy in ministry at that church. Paul then went on to preach in Macedonia, where he heard reports of Timothy's work at Ephesus that prompted him to write 1 Timothy, probably in AD 63.

Why Is First Timothy so Important?

First Timothy presents the most explicit and complete instructions for church leadership and organization in the entire Bible. This includes sections on appropriate conduct in worship gatherings, the qualifications of elders and deacons, and the proper order of church discipline. Paul advised Timothy on these practical matters in a way that would have helped the young pastor to emphasize the purity that should characterize Christian leaders and the gatherings they oversee.

What's the Big Idea?

Timothy's youth no doubt served him well, allowing for the energy and vigor he needed to serve his people. However, it also caused inevitable difficulties with older Christians who may not have taken quickly to the leadership of such a young man because of his lack of knowledge and experience in leadership. It was important to Paul that Timothy set an example of consistent faith and a good conscience, remaining above reproach and exercising the spiritual gifts that God had given him (1 Timothy 4:12–16).

However, Paul knew that such a task would not be easy for the young man. Therefore, on two occasions Paul encouraged Timothy to "fight the good fight" (1:18; 6:12). Perseverance in what was good often became a slog for Timothy, one that required thick skin and a clear purpose.

How Do I Apply This?

The leaders of our churches fill important roles as they participate in encouraging the spiritual growth of Christians under their care. We know the significance of these men in our churches and in our personal lives, but 1 Timothy helps us to gain a clearer understanding of the proper qualifications and roles for church leaders. Paul's letter shows us those things he hoped Timothy would address in his ministry, providing a template of sorts that our leaders can follow in their own ministries.

How do your leaders implement Paul's exhortations in 1 Timothy? Our churches will be strongest when they are closest to the biblical vision laid out for them. As you look at your church or look for a new one, consider the priorities of the leaders. Look for an emphasis on sound doctrine, on purity within the leaders' personal lives, and on living out the Christian faith by example. Find those qualities, and you will more than likely find a church where you can thrive.

FIRST TIMOTHY

Greeting (1:1–2)

Conclusion (6:21)

	Personal Encouragement and Exhortation	The Ministry	The Minister
	Timothy's task	Men and women (2) (Prayer and submission)	**Seeing the importance of (4):** Faithful teaching — True godliness / Sound doctrine — Perseverance
	Paul's testimony		**Paying attention to (5):**
	Gospel's trustworthiness	Elders and deacons (3) (Qualifications for leadership)	Various age groups — Elders / Widows — Wisdom
			Developing a new perspective toward (6): Masters and slaves — Internals and externals / Rich and poor — Eternal vs. temporal
	CHAPTER 1	*CHAPTERS 2–3*	*CHAPTERS 4–6*
Emphasis	The work of ministry		The one who ministers
Command	Be true!	Be wise!	Be strong and faithful!
Theme	Leadership of the church, the household of God		
Key Verses		3:14–15	
Christ in 1 Timothy	Jesus is the Mediator between God and people, the ransom for all, who came in the flesh and was taken up in glory (2:5–6; 3:16).		

SECOND TIMOTHY

—❧❧—

Who Wrote the Book?

By the time Paul wrote his second letter to Timothy, the young pastor had
been ministering to the church at Ephesus for four years, and it had been
almost that long since he had received his first letter from Paul. Timothy
had been a faithful servant to Paul since he had left home with the
apostle more than a decade earlier. Since then, Timothy had ministered
alongside Paul for the duration of both the second and third missionary
journeys, in places such as Troas, Philippi, and Corinth. Timothy was
not unfamiliar to the Ephesians when he settled in Ephesus to minister,
having served there alongside Paul for a period of close to three years on
Paul's third missionary journey. Paul wrote again to this young leader in
the church at Ephesus to provide him encouragement and fortitude in
the face of difficulties and trials.

Where Are We?

Paul wrote 2 Timothy from a dark and damp Roman prison cell, just
before his death in AD 67. The Roman emperor Nero had been slowly
descending into madness since his ascent to the throne in AD 54, a
process exacerbated by the great fire of Rome in AD 64 that burned half
the city. With the residents of Rome in an uproar, Christians became a
convenient target for Nero, who used believers as scapegoats for his city's
own lack of preparedness. Paul was one of those caught up in this
persecution and was beheaded by Roman officials soon after writing
this letter.

Why Is Second Timothy so Important?

The second letter to Timothy offers a picture of Paul at the end of his ministry, just before his death. Certain personal details in the letter reveal a man settling his accounts and preparing for the inevitable. At the close of the letter, Paul mentioned a significant number of people—some who had wronged him and others who had served faithfully alongside him (2 Timothy 4:9–21). It is as if Paul were giving Timothy a "state of the church" address, updating Timothy on the current state of their acquaintances and friends so that the young pastor could carry on after Paul's departure.

What's the Big Idea?

Paul understood that the ministry would only become more difficult for Timothy with the apostle's impending death. (Indeed, at some point after this letter from Paul, Timothy was imprisoned for his faith [Hebrews 13:23]). Paul knew that Timothy's task of keeping the church within the bounds of sound doctrine while encouraging believers to live their lives well for the sake of Christ would be an often thankless and difficult task. Though hardship would come, Paul wanted Timothy to continue in those things he had learned, drawing on the rich heritage of faith that had been passed down to the young pastor, not just from Paul but also from his mother and grandmother (2 Timothy 1:5–6; 3:14–15).

The most striking feature of Paul's encouragement comes when the aging apostle used a phrase that showed up prominently in his letter to Timothy four years prior. In that earlier letter, Paul exhorted Timothy to "fight the good fight" (1 Timothy 1:18; 6:12). But in this letter, Paul turned that phrase on himself, writing that he had "fought the good fight . . . finished the course . . . [and] kept the faith" (2 Timothy 4:7). What a great encouragement it must have been to the young pastor of the church at Ephesus to know that his mentor boldly modeled his perseverance in the faith, even to the point of death.

How Do I Apply This?

Second Timothy brings us to the brink of death, forcing us to consider its reality and how we might react when faced with it. Paul's response instructs us still today. His mind was not on himself, dwelling on the injustice that had befallen him. Instead, trusting that God had him right where He wanted him, the aging apostle turned his attention to others, specifically to the church and to his young protégé, Timothy.

Where do you hope your thoughts linger as you come to the end of your days?

SECOND TIMOTHY

	Guard the Treasure!	Suffer Hardship!	Continue!	Preach the Word!
	Paul's greeting Timothy's life God's treasure Our responsibility	Passing on the truth Illustrations of the truth (soldier, athlete, farmer, workman, vessel, servant) Suffering for the truth	Last days Evil people Standing firm Biblical basis Spiritual examples	A solemn charge Reason for the charge Personal conclusion
	CHAPTER 1	CHAPTER 2	CHAPTER 3	CHAPTER 4
Perspective	The past	The present	The future	
Tone	Gratitude	Compassion	Warning	Command
Theme	Paul's passing of the ministry torch to Timothy and encouraging him to stay faithful in the midst of hardship			
Key Verses	1:14	2:3	3:14	4:2
Christ in 2 Timothy	Jesus is the Judge of the living and the dead, who strengthens us in times of weakness and rescues us in times of danger (3:11; 4:1, 17).			

TITUS

—❦—

Who Wrote the Book?

Paul identified himself as the author of the letter to Titus, calling himself a "bond-servant of God and an apostle of Jesus Christ" (Titus 1:1). The origin of Paul's relationship with Titus is shrouded in mystery, though we can gather that he may have been converted under the ministry of Paul, who called Titus "my true child in a common faith" (1:4). Titus accompanied Paul on his third missionary journey, during which the apostle sent him to Corinth at least once (2 Corinthians 2:12–13; 7:5–7, 13–15; 8:6, 16–24). Paul clearly held Titus in a position of great respect as a friend and fellow worker for the gospel, praising Titus for his affection, his earnestness, and his bringing comfort to others.

Where Are We?

Paul wrote his letter to Titus from Nicopolis in AD 63, after the apostle's release from his first Roman imprisonment. Upon leaving Timothy in Ephesus to minister there, Paul accompanied Titus to the island of Crete, where he intended Titus to lead and organize the island's churches in their early years of existence. While the gospel had no doubt spread to Crete soon after Peter's sermon at Pentecost (Acts 2:11), Paul and Titus likely did a good deal of evangelism on the island in the weeks before Paul commissioned Titus to a leadership position there.

Why Is Titus so Important?

Three summaries of the incarnation dot the pages of Titus, providing a framework within which the Christian can view the work of God in the world and in individual lives (Titus 1:1–4; 2:11–14; 3:4–7). All three passages involve the manifestation, or appearance, of God in Christ, rooting the Christian faith in the incarnation of Jesus Christ. Only when God the Son took on human flesh in the person of Jesus was the believer's faith in God made sure. In other words, since God poured out His grace on all humanity, He cleanses His people from their sin and purifies believers for Himself. This grace of God instructs us to live upright and godly lives in this present age (2:11–3:8).

What's the Big Idea?

The doctrine of the incarnation in the letter to Titus grounds its message of producing right living through the careful attention to theological truth. The churches on Crete were just as susceptible to false teachers as any other church, so Paul directed Titus to establish a group of faithful elders to oversee the doctrinal purity and good conduct of the believers on Crete. Paul exhorted Titus to "speak the things which are fitting for sound doctrine" (Titus 2:1), a clear direction that this should be the young pastor's primary role.

However, Paul also understood that when a body of believers embraces sound doctrine, the result is changed and purified lives that produce "good deeds" (mentioned in Titus 2:7, 14; 3:8, 14). God's grace is the motivation for all good deeds. Paul gave instructions to Titus about the roles of specific groups of people—older men, older women, young women, young men, and slaves—as well as general instructions to all believers about their conduct. Right living was essential because Christ "gave Himself for us to redeem us from every lawless deed," saving us "by the washing of regeneration and renewing by the Holy Spirit" (Titus 2:14; 3:5).

How Do I Apply This?

How seriously do you consider your beliefs about God in the overall scheme of your life? The book of Titus reminds us that our beliefs about God impact every decision we make. Sometimes it is difficult for believers today to see the point of getting all worked up about the person and nature of Christ or the doctrine of the Trinity. However, Paul made clear that a church that teaches and preaches sound doctrine will see results in the lives of its people. Not only will people be saved from their sins, but God's grace will also motivate them to live out that saving faith with renewed and purified lives.

Many churches today focus more on the form of their worship—music styles, lighting, and building designs—than they do on the content of the faith they mean to proclaim. And while the form of a church's worship is vital to reaching its community for Christ, without a firm base of sound doctrine, the church will lay its foundation in shifting and sinking sand. Make doctrine a priority in your own life, as well as encouraging it in your churches. Nothing is more significant than a solid foundation in Christ. Nothing is more motivational than grace to live a life of good deeds.

TITUS

Introduction (1:1–4) | Conclusion (3:12–15)

	Taking Charge		**Giving Advice**	**Doing Right**
	Elders		Older men and women	What to do
	Rebellious people		Young women and men	What not to do
			Titus and all leaders	
			Slaves and masters	
	CHAPTER 1		CHAPTER 2	CHAPTER 3
People	Elders	Enemies	Specific groups	Christians in general
Issue	Setting up the right leadership		Instruction for particular people	Attitude and conduct toward good and bad
A Church	. . . in good order (1:5)		. . . with good doctrine (2:1)	. . . of good deeds (3:1)
Theme	Titus's role in encouraging right living through sound doctrine			
Key Verses	1:5; 2:10; 3:8			
Christ in Titus	Jesus is our great God and Savior, who redeems and purifies His people (2:13–14).			

PHILEMON

Who Wrote the Book?

For more than two years during his third missionary journey, Paul ministered in Asia Minor among the people of Ephesus. This was a successful period for the apostle to the Gentiles, who saw many converts among both residents of Ephesus and visitors to the city. One of the visitors converted under Paul's teaching was a man named Philemon, a slave-owner from the nearby city of Colossae (Philemon 1:19). In the Bible book that bears Philemon's name, Paul addressed his "beloved brother" as a "fellow worker," a title given to those who served for a time alongside Paul. (Gospel writers Mark and Luke also received this title later in the letter [1:1, 24]). Clearly, a kinship existed between Paul and Philemon, one that would serve a significant purpose in light of the circumstance that brought about the letter.

Where Are We?

A slave named Onesimus had escaped from his owner, Philemon, and had run away from Colossae to Rome in the hope that he could disappear into that populous, urban environment. Once in Rome, Onesimus, either by accident or by his own design, came in contact with Paul, who promptly led the runaway slave to faith in Jesus Christ. Paul had already been planning to send a letter to the Colossian church by the hand of Tychicus. So in AD 60 or 61 from a prison cell in Rome, Paul wrote a personal letter to Philemon and sent Onesimus the slave back to Colossae.

Why Is Philemon so Important?

The letter to Philemon reminds us that God's revelation to humanity is intensely personal. In more formal biblical works such as the Gospels or the epistle to the Romans or even Paul's letters to churches at Philippi or Colossae, it might be easy to get the impression that God does not care or have time for the trials and tribulations in a single household. Philemon stands as one piece of strong evidence to the contrary, revealing that lofty doctrines such as the love of God, forgiveness in Christ, or the inherent dignity of humanity have real and pertinent impact in everyday life. The book of Philemon illustrates that principles like these can and should profoundly affect the lives of believers.

What's the Big Idea?

Paul's message to Philemon was a simple one: based on the work of love and forgiveness that had been wrought in Philemon's heart by God, show the same to the escaped and now-believing slave Onesimus. The apostle's message would have had extra force behind it because he knew Philemon personally. Paul had explained the gospel to Philemon and had witnessed the profound result: new life blossoming in a once-dead heart (Philemon 1:19). Paul knew that conversion is nothing to trifle with, but that it should be honored and fostered.

So Paul made a request. He wanted Philemon to forgive Onesimus, to accept the slave as a brother in Christ, and to consider sending Onesimus back to Paul, as the apostle found him useful in God's service (1:11–14). Paul did not minimize Onesimus's sin. This was not some kind of cheap grace that Paul asked Philemon to offer. No, there was sacrifice required in this request, and because of that, Paul approached the topic with gentleness and care (1:21). His letter to Philemon presents in full color the beautiful and majestic transition from slavery to kinship that comes as a result of Christian love and forgiveness.

How Do I Apply This?

Live long enough, and you will understand the difficulty of offering forgiveness when you have been wronged. It does not come easy, yet as believers, we have to recognize that our ability and willingness to offer it are the result of Christ's saving work on the cross. Because of that fact, forgiveness serves as a determining factor in who we say we are and how we hope to live our lives. When we do not forgive, bitterness takes root in our hearts and chokes the vitality out of us.

In what ways has forgiveness been a struggle for you since you accepted Christ's forgiveness? Allow Paul's letter to Philemon to encourage forgiveness in your own life, and trust God to foster renewed life in your heart and your relationships.

PHILEMON

	Greeting (1:1–3)	Paul's Commendation	Paul's Request	Paul's Promise	Conclusion (1:21–25)
			On the basis of the slave's conversion (1:8–11)		
			On the basis of the slave owner's friendship (1:12–17)		
		VERSES 4–7	*VERSES 8–17*	*VERSES 18–21*	
Tone		Praise	Plea	Promise	
Direction		Looking back	Looking within	Looking beyond	
Central Statement		"I thank my God always." (1:4)	"I appeal to you." (1:10)	"I will repay it." (1:19)	
Theme		Forgiving and accepting one another as brothers and sisters in Christ			
Key Verses			1:10–11, 15–18		
Christ in Philemon		Jesus is the Master, in whom believers are brothers and sisters in Christ (1:9, 15–16).			

78

THE
GENERAL EPISTLES

Eight letters comprise the group of books we know as the General Epistles. Made up of books from a variety of authors—including James and Jude, who were half-brothers of Jesus, and Peter and John, who were disciples of Jesus—these were letters sent to churches all across the Roman Empire to instruct believers in the faith and guide them in their practice of Christianity. These letters contain some of the most intimate and important instruction in all the New Testament—from the supremacy of Christ to the nature of believers' fellowship with God and others.

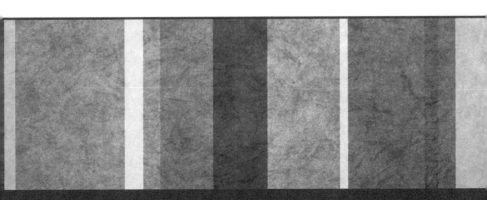

HEBREWS

—✦—

Who Wrote the Book?

The author of the letter to the Hebrews remains shrouded in mystery. Even early in the church's history, a Christian as learned as Origen had to admit his ignorance of the true author of Hebrews. Several theories regarding the author's identity have been proposed over the years, but all of them contain significant problems.

Most of the churches in the eastern part of the Roman Empire believed Paul to have authored the book, leading to its early acceptance into the Canon by the churches in those areas. Even though Clement of Rome drew much from Hebrews in his late-first-century letter to the Corinthian church, many in the Western church pointed away from Paul as the source of the book. Authors such as Luke, Barnabas, Apollos, and even Clement have been considered as possibilities. The unknown authorship of this book should not shake our confidence in its authority. Hebrews makes important theological contributions to the biblical Canon, it has been drawn upon as sacred Scripture since the late first century, and Christians have for two millennia consistently upheld the divine inspiration and, therefore, the canonicity of the book of Hebrews.

Where Are We?

The strongly Jewish character of the letter to the Hebrews helps to narrow down its date of composition, most likely AD 64–69. Significantly, the book makes no reference to the destruction of the temple at Jerusalem in AD 70, and the author wrote as if the sacrificial system were still in existence (Hebrews 10:1–2, 11). With its myriad references to Hebrew customs and the Old Testament, the book was likely sent to a Jewish Christian community, possibly in Rome.

Why Is Hebrews so Important?

Hebrews clearly lays out the present priestly ministry of Christ in the life of the believer. Jesus is both the divine Son of God and completely human, and in His priestly role He clears the way for human beings to approach the Father in heaven through prayer (Hebrews 4:14–16). The priesthood of Jesus is superior to the Old Testament priesthood of Aaron, because only through Jesus do we receive eternal salvation (5:1–9). Furthermore, Jesus became the permanent and perfect High Priest, going beyond all other priests by offering Himself as a sinless sacrifice on behalf of the sins of human beings (7:24–26; 9:28).

What's the Big Idea?

Throughout its pages, Hebrews makes clear that Jesus Christ exceeds all other people, pursuits, objects, or hopes to which human beings offer allegiance. Hebrews pictures Jesus as better than the angels, as bringing better lives to humanity through salvation, as offering a better hope than the Mosaic Law could promise, as a better sacrifice for our sins than a bull or a goat, and as providing a better inheritance in heaven for those who place their faith in Him (Hebrews 1:4; 6:9; 7:19; 9:23; 10:34). Jesus is indeed superior to all others.

This message of the superiority of Jesus would have been particularly important to Jewish Christians in Rome, who were struggling under Nero's persecution and were considering moving back toward the Mosaic Law. The writer to the Hebrews showed these Jewish Christian believers that, though they were faced with suffering, they were indeed following a better way . . . and they should persevere.

How Do I Apply This?

The ancients created idols fashioned of wood and stone. Modern society has set aside that type of idol in favor of new idols—idols of fancy gadgets, material wealth, a comfortable lifestyle, and even our children. Human beings have seen and experienced the limitless bounty of idolatry, where we place some created object or person in the place of the one true God. What idols do you hold dear in your life?

The letter to the Hebrews makes clear that only one Person deserves to hold the primary place in our lives. While we are busy idolizing our move up the corporate ladder or placing all our hopes in our kids, Jesus offers us a better position, a better priest, a better covenant, a better hope, and a better sacrifice.

Only when we give Jesus His rightful place in our lives will everything else in life fall into its rightful place.

HEBREWS

Prologue (1:1–4)

Epilogue (13:20–25)

	Jesus Christ: Superior in His Person		Jesus Christ: Superior as Our Priest		Jesus Christ: Superior for Life
	Superior to: Prophets Angels Moses The Sabbath Other priests		**Better than:** Earthly priesthood Old covenant (Mosaic system) Animal sacrifices Daily offerings		**Let us have:** Faith to believe God Hope to endure trials Love to encourage others
	CHAPTERS 1:1–4:13		CHAPTERS 4:14–10:18		CHAPTERS 10:19–13:25
Emphasis	Instruction				Exhortation
Key Words	"Much better than" 1:4		"Better" 7:19		"Let us" 12:1
Warnings	2:1–4	3:7–4:13	5:11–6:20	10:19–39	12:25–29
Theme	The absolute superiority of Jesus Christ				
Key Verse	4:14				
Christ in Hebrews	Jesus is the absolutely superior revelation of God and our eternal High Priest (1:1–14; 3:1).				

JAMES

———❧———

Who Wrote the Book?

While James did not specifically identify himself as to which "James" he was (James 1:1), the author is widely thought to be James the half-brother of Jesus. James was not a follower of Jesus during the Savior's time on earth (Mark 3:21–35; John 7:5) but eventually became an apostle in the vein of Paul, as one who had seen and believed the Lord post-resurrection (1 Corinthians 15:7; Galatians 1:19). After witnessing the Lord's resurrected body, James became one of the leaders of the church at Jerusalem. Peter singled him out among the other Christians there following Peter's miraculous release from prison (Acts 12:17). James made the deciding speech at the Jerusalem Council (15:13–22), and Paul called James one of the pillars of the church (Galatians 2:9).

Where Are We?

As one of the chief leaders in the church at Jerusalem, James wrote from that city prior to the meeting of the Jerusalem Council, which Luke recorded in Acts 15. At that council, James, along with Peter and Paul, affirmed the decision to take the gospel message to the Gentiles. This council met in AD 49, meaning James likely wrote his letter in AD 45–48. Such a significant event as the Jerusalem Council warranted comment from James, as he was writing to a Jewish Christian audience. But James made no mention of Gentile Christians at all, making an early date for the letter most likely. In fact, it was likely the first New Testament book written.

Why Is James so Important?

The book of James looks a bit like the Old Testament book of Proverbs dressed up in New Testament clothes. Its consistent focus on practical action in the life of faith is reminiscent of the Wisdom Literature in the Old Testament, encouraging God's people to *act* like God's people. The pages of James are filled with direct commands to pursue a life of holiness. He makes no excuses for those who do not measure up. In the mind of this early church leader, Christians evidence their faith by walking in certain ways and not others. For James, a faith that does not produce real life change is a faith that is worthless (James 2:17).

What's the Big Idea?

In the opening of his letter, James called himself a bond-servant of God, an appropriate name given the practical, servant-oriented emphasis of the book. Throughout the book, James contended that faith produces authentic deeds. In other words, if those who call themselves God's people truly belong to Him, their lives will produce deeds or fruit. In language and themes that sound similar to Jesus's Sermon on the Mount, James rails against the hypocritical believer who says one thing but does another.

For James, faith was no abstract proposition but had effects in the real world. James offered numerous practical examples to illustrate his point: faith endures in the midst of trials, calls on God for wisdom, bridles the tongue, sets aside wickedness, visits orphans and widows, and does not play favorites. He stressed that the life of faith is comprehensive, impacting every area of our lives and driving us to truly engage in the lives of other people in the world. While James recognized that even believers stumble (James 3:2), he also knew that faith should not coexist with people who roll their eyes at the less fortunate, ignore the plight of others, or curse those in their paths.

How Do I Apply This?

More than any other book in the New Testament, James places the spotlight on the necessity for believers to act in accordance with our faith. How well do your actions mirror the faith that you proclaim? This is a question that we all struggle to answer well. We would like to point to all the ways our faith and works overlap but too often see only gaps and crevices.

As you read the letter from James, focus on those areas that he mentioned: your actions during trials, your treatment of those less fortunate, the way you speak and relate to others, and the role that money plays in how you live your life. Allow James to encourage you to do good, according to the faith you proclaim.

JAMES

	When stretched, it doesn't break.	When pressed, it doesn't fail.	When expressed, it doesn't explode.	When distressed, it doesn't panic.
Faith				
Deeds	Authentic stability	Authentic love	Authentic control and humility	Authentic patience
	Greeting	Partiality and prejudice	The tongue	Money matters
	Trials	Indifference and mere intellectualism	The heart	Sickness
	Temptation	Obedience and action	The will	Carnality and correction
	Response to Scripture			
	CHAPTER 1	*CHAPTER 2*	*CHAPTERS 3–4*	*CHAPTER 5*

Background	The difficulties of life caused the scattered saints to drift spiritually, leading to all forms of problems—unbridled speech, wrong attitudes, doubt, strife, carnality, shallow faith.
Characteristics	"The Proverbs of the New Testament," James contains many practical, straightforward exhortations. Emphasis is on importance of balancing right belief with right behavior. The book has many Old Testament word pictures and references.
Theme	Real faith produces authentic deeds.
Key Verse	2:17
Christ in James	Jesus is the glorious Lord, who inspires true faith and authentic works (2:1, 14–26).

FIRST PETER

Who Wrote the Book?

The first word of this epistle, *Peter*, identifies the author, who called himself "an apostle of Jesus Christ" (1 Peter 1:1). He wrote this letter to a group of Christians scattered throughout the northern areas of Asia Minor, where he may have previously preached the gospel.

Peter wrote to a group of people that probably included both Jews and Gentiles. The apostle addressed the letter's recipients as "aliens" (1:1), a word indicating that Peter was speaking not just to Jews or just to Gentiles but to Christians who were living their lives in such a way that they would have stood out as aliens among the surrounding culture.

Where Are We?

In this letter, Peter spoke much about persecution, which anticipated the persecution he and other Christians would endure in the final years of Nero's reign. At the time he wrote, Peter had not yet been arrested, an event that would lead to his martyrdom around AD 66–68. First Peter 5:13 indicates that Peter sent greetings from the local church—calling it "Babylon"—but it's most likely that the apostle was writing in a common metaphor there. He used the name of the ancient Mesopotamian city as a stand-in for Rome, the modern city that, like Babylon, gave itself over to idol worship and false gods. While the fact is not recorded in the Bible, Peter has long been thought to have spent his final years serving the church in Rome. Based on the numerous references to suffering and persecution in this letter, Peter likely wrote in AD 64, just as the persecution of Christians under Nero was ramping up.

Why Is First Peter so Important?

First Peter focuses on the importance of believers bearing up under unjust suffering yet continuing to live well (1 Peter 2:20). In this way, 1 Peter might be called the Job of the New Testament, providing encouragement for the true believer to continue on in the way that Jesus has laid out for all His followers. The endurance Peter called these believers to is similar to Job's, a man who suffered despite his righteousness. Peter maintained that this was the kind of true perseverance that God expects from His people.

What's the Big Idea?

Living in close proximity to Jesus Christ for more than three years had provided the apostle Peter the best possible example of what it looked like to live in holiness amid a hostile world. More than any other man who walked the earth, Jesus modeled that lifestyle. Peter therefore pointed his readers in the best possible direction, to Jesus Himself. The apostle called Christians to "sanctify Christ as Lord" in their hearts, that believers might live and act as Jesus desires during their short time here on earth (1 Peter 3:14–18). This would include submission to authority—even unjust authority—in the government, in the home, and in the workplace. Jesus becomes the focal point for ordering one's life in the midst of trials and tribulations. By rooting their perseverance in the person and work of Christ, believers can always cling to hope in the midst of suffering.

How Do I Apply This?

Unjust or unforeseen suffering is one of the great problems that grips the hearts of people today. We struggle with frustration, anger, and uncertainty when trials strange and unexpected land on our doorsteps. Too often in those most difficult moments of our lives, confusion reigns while contentment wanes; questions arise while prayer subsides.

How do you react when suffering comes? Many crumble at the mere thought of another pain or trial. Others rise to the occasion. Most of us are probably somewhere in between. Peter's encouragement to his Christian readers is one of perseverance in faith. It isn't enough for us to simply get up every morning and trudge through each day; neither is it advisable to paste a smile on our faces and ignore troubles. Instead, the lesson of 1 Peter is to push through the troubles, recognizing their temporary presence in our lives while walking in holiness and hope as people of faith.

So press on! It is in the darkest times that our collective light shines brightest.

FIRST PETER

	Our Living Hope and Holy Life	Our Submission and God's Honor	Our Suffering and Christ's Suffering
Salutation (1:1–2)	"Blessed be the God and Father of our Lord Jesus Christ" (1:3) . . . for the hope we claim (1:3–12) . . . by our walk of holiness (1:13–25) . . . for our new identity in Christ (2:1–12)	"Submit yourselves for the Lord's sake" (2:13) . . . to the government (2:13–17) . . . at work (2:18–20) . . . like Christ (2:21–25) . . . in the home (3:1–7)	"Since Christ has suffered" (4:1) Keep a good conscience (3:16) Share the sufferings and rejoice (4:13) Commit yourselves to God (4:19) Be humble (5:6) Cast your anxiety on God (5:7)	Conclusion (5:12–14)
	CHAPTERS 1:3–2:12	*CHAPTERS 2:13–3:7*	*CHAPTERS 3:8–5:11*

Emphasis	Informing	Exhorting	Encouraging
Grace	. . . to go on	. . . to live faithfully	. . . to stand firm
Hope	A *living* hope through Christ's resurrection (1:3)	A *righteous* hope through personal submission (2:15)	A *trusting* hope through faith (4:19)
Theme	Holy living in a hostile world; hope in the midst of suffering		
Key Verses	1:3–5, 13–16; 2:21; 4:12–13, 19; 5:10–11		
Christ in 1 Peter	Jesus is the living stone rejected by men, who has become the Cornerstone of the church and the Shepherd of our souls (2:4–10, 25).		

SECOND PETER

Who Wrote the Book?

Peter introduced himself at the beginning of the letter as "a bond-servant and apostle of Jesus Christ," and he addressed the letter "to those who have received a faith of the same kind as ours" (2 Peter 1:1). Only later does it become apparent that Peter was writing to the same group of believers who had received his first letter. In 2 Peter 3:1, the author reflected that this is "the second letter I am writing to you."

Much ink has been spilled in modern times over the question of whether or not Peter was in fact the author of this book—the authorship of 2 Peter being the most disputed in the New Testament. But the burden of proof is always on those who doubt the direct reference in the letter's first verse, and despite their efforts, scholars have not been able to marshal arguments persuasive enough for the wise believer to doubt the inspiration and inerrancy of Scripture and dismiss the revelation of 2 Peter 1:1.

Where Are We?

Peter wrote this letter from Rome soon after he wrote 1 Peter in AD 64–66. So what would have prompted another letter to the same group so soon after the first? From the contents of the letter, it appears that Peter had received reports of false teachers in and among the churches in Asia Minor. The apostle warned them about the insidious presence of those who spread heresies among the people (2 Peter 2:1), marking such difficulties as a sign of the last days (3:3). Peter wanted to encourage his people to stand firm and to instruct them on how best to do that.

Why Is Second Peter so Important?

The churches of Asia Minor were not just struggling with the persecution and suffering addressed in Peter's first letter; they also had strife and dissension within their ranks. In an effort to stem the tide of heresy and false teaching among the Christians, Peter emphasized the importance of learning and clinging to the proper knowledge of God. In fact, this concept was so important to him that the word *knowledge* appears—in one form or another—some fifteen times in the span of this short, three-chapter letter.

What's the Big Idea?

Peter's theme in his second letter is a simple one: pursue spiritual maturity through the Word of God as a remedy for false teaching and a right response to heretics in light of Christ's promised second coming (2 Peter 1:3, 16). When false teachers begin to whisper their sweet words into the ears of immature Christians, the body of Christ begins to break apart, to lose what makes it distinctive in the first place—faith in the unique person and work of Jesus Christ. Peter repeatedly points to the Word of God as the primary means of growth for the Christian (1:4, 19–21; 3:1–2, 14–16).

Peter encouraged his readers to apply themselves to acquiring the true knowledge of God and living out the life of faith with "all diligence," so that they may "be found by [Jesus] in peace, spotless and blameless" (1:5; 3:14). And if believers did not follow his advice, they would be giving their Christian community over to the heretics, people who look to "exploit . . . with false words" (2:3).

How Do I Apply This?

As with the recipients of Peter's letter, we all go through difficult times. Those trials seem to hit us even harder when the source of the struggles comes from somewhere or someone close to us. We know intuitively this is true in our personal lives: a rift in a marriage, an unwed daughter's unexpected pregnancy, or an abusive relationship with a relative. But it holds true within the church as well.

Believers can create dissension in multiple ways, particularly in the areas of relationships and theology. To guard against that kind of discord—both in our families and our churches—God's people need to know who He is. Our knowledge of God through His Word is the first line of defense against the conflicts that threaten to tear us apart. As Peter wrote: "Be on your guard so that you are not carried away by the error of unprincipled men . . . but grow in the grace and knowledge of our Lord and Savior Jesus Christ" (2 Peter 3:17–18).

With that in mind, what means are you taking to grow in your faith? Let's take the time to guard our minds with the proper knowledge of God so that we may not drift off from the path that God has laid out for us.

SECOND PETER

	Exhortation to Spiritual Maturity	Denunciation of False Teachers	Anticipation of Christ's Return
	Answers question: How can I grow in grace and knowledge? (1:2–3)	**Answers question:** What should I expect from so-called prophets?	**Answers question:** What sort of people ought we to be? (3:11)
	CHAPTER 1	CHAPTER 2	CHAPTER 3
Warning	Be pure! (1:4)	Be aware! (2:1–3)	Be diligent! (3:1–14)
Reminder	1:12–13	2:21–22	3:1–2
Promise	"You will never stumble." (1:10)	"The Lord knows how to rescue." (2:9)	"We are looking for new heavens and a new earth." (3:13)
Perspective	Looking within	Looking back	Looking ahead
Theme	Spiritual maturity as a remedy for false teaching and a right response in light of Christ's second coming		
Key Verses	3:17–18		
Christ in 2 Peter	Jesus is the Morning Star, who rescues the righteous from temptation and reserves the wicked for judgment (1:19; 2:9).		

FIRST JOHN

—✦—

Who Wrote the Book?

The author of this epistle never identified himself by name, but Christians since the beginning of the church have considered this letter authoritative, believing it was written by John the apostle. That group of witnesses includes Polycarp, an early second-century bishop who as a young man knew John personally. In addition, the author clearly places himself as part of a group of apostolic eyewitnesses to the life and ministry of Jesus, noting that "what we have seen and heard we proclaim to you also" (1 John 1:3).

Where Are We?

John did not specify the recipients of this letter, but given his addresses in Revelation 2–3 to seven churches in the immediate vicinity of Ephesus—the city where John ministered late in his life—he likely had those same churches in mind for this letter. The letter offers little in the way of specifics, so pinpointing the date of its composition can be difficult. However, its similarity with the gospel composed by John means it was probably written near the same time. A date of about AD 90, with John writing from his exile on Patmos, ends up being the best proposition.

Why Is First John so Important?

The parallelisms in 1 John are striking for their simplicity: Christ vs. antichrists, light vs. darkness, truth vs. falsehood, righteousness vs. sin, love of the Father vs. love of the world, and the Spirit of God vs. the spirit of the Antichrist. While this is not a complete list, it reveals a letter that presents the world in an uncomplicated way—there is right and there is wrong, period. This emphasis by John, while striking, is not without love. It's quite the opposite, in fact. John recognized that love comes from God, and he encouraged the believers to love one another (1 John 4:7). John's first epistle teaches that while it is important to recognize the lines between truth and error, it must always be done in a spirit of love.

What's the Big Idea?

As he did in his gospel, John stated with clarity the purpose of his first letter. He proclaimed the good news about Jesus to the recipients of this letter, saying "so that you too may have fellowship with us; and indeed our fellowship is with the Father, and with His Son Jesus Christ" (1 John 1:3). Later, John added "so that you may not sin" (2:1) and "so that you may know that you have eternal life" (5:13). John wanted his readers to experience true fellowship with God and with God's people. But he knew that would not happen until the Christians set aside their own selfish desires in favor of the pursuits God had for them.

To help them attain that goal, John focused on three issues: the zeal of the believers, standing firm against false teachers, and reassuring the Christians that they have eternal life. John wrote to churches full of people who had struggled with discouragement—whether due to their own sinful failures or the presence of false teachers in their midst. The aging apostle hoped to ignite the zeal of these believers so that they might follow the Lord more closely and stand firm against those who meant to sow discord among the churches. In doing so, they would solidify their relationship with God and gain confidence in His work in their lives.

How Do I Apply This?

We all go through ups and downs in our Christian faith. Whatever the struggle—whether outside of us or inside—we often feel ourselves blown about by the winds of emotion or circumstances. Yet God calls us to lives of increasing consistency, with the evidence of our inner transformation becoming more and more apparent as the months and years pass by. How would you characterize your relationship with God—consistent and fruitful or sporadic and parched?

John knew that we would never find in ourselves the faithfulness God requires. Instead, we have to place complete trust in the work and grace of God, believing that He will certainly conform us to the image of His Son, Jesus. That sense of being grounded in God only comes when we set aside our sin in the pursuit of the one true God. Or, in the words of John, "if we love one another, God abides in us, and His love is perfected in us" (1 John 4:12).

FIRST JOHN

Prologue (1:1–4)		Walking with the God of Light		Responding to the God of Love			
		Living in the Light	Staying in the Light	Practicing the Righteousness and Love of God	Testing the Spirits	Loving Others as God Loved Us	Believing in Jesus
		CHAPTERS 1:5–2:11	CHAPTER 2:12–27	CHAPTERS 2:28–3:23	CHAPTERS 3:24–4:6	CHAPTER 4:7–21	CHAPTER 5
Fellowship with God Produces a . . .		Clean life	Discerning life		Loving life		Confident life
Emphasis		Light	Truth		Love		Knowledge
Means		Obeying	Perceiving		Sacrificing		Believing
Christ		Advocate (2:1)	Holy One (2:20)	Son of God (3:8)		Savior of the world (4:14)	
Purposes		That we may have fellowship and joy (1:3–4)	That we may not sin (2:1)	That we may not be deceived (2:26)			That we may know that we have eternal life (5:13)
Theme		Living in fellowship with God, who is light and love					
Key Verses		1:5–7		4:10–16		5:11–13	
Christ in 1 John		Jesus is the Word of Life, who is God come in the flesh to bring eternal life to those who believe (1:1; 4:2; 5:20).					

SECOND JOHN

Who Wrote the Book?

John did not identify himself by name in this letter, but he did adopt the term "elder" for himself (2 John 1:1). There has been some debate about whether an author named John the Elder wrote this letter (as well as 3 John, which is addressed the same way) or if John the apostle was using a different title for himself. However, the earliest church tradition from the second century on testified in unison that this letter and its companion, 3 John, were written by the apostle, not by a mysterious and unknown elder. In fact, an apostle using the term "elder" for himself was not at all unprecedented—Peter did that very thing in his first epistle (1 Peter 5:1).

Where Are We?

John offered little in the way of detail in the short letter we call 2 John. Nothing in the circumstances John discussed in the letter would lead a reader of the time to think that it did not go to the same churches that received 1 John. The apostle addressed the letter "to the chosen lady and her children," a mysterious phrase that has been much debated (2 John 1:1). It either refers to an actual woman or serves as a metaphor for a church. In either case, whether to a smaller family group joined by blood or to a larger one joined by confession, the application of the letter should remain unchanged. With this letter's thematic similarity to 1 John, it is best to suggest that John wrote from Patmos in about AD 90.

Why Is Second John so Important?

Second John makes clear what our position should be regarding the enemies of the truth. Whereas 1 John focuses on our fellowship with God, 2 John focuses on protecting our fellowship from those who teach falsehood. The apostle went so far as to warn his readers against inviting false teachers into the house or even offering them a greeting (2 John 1:10). Such practices align the believer with the evildoer, and John was keen on keeping the believers pure from the stain of falsehood and heresy.

What's the Big Idea?

John began his second epistle proclaiming his love for "the chosen lady and her children," a love he shared with those who know the truth (2 John 1:1). From the reports he had received, he understood that these believers were following the teachings of Christ. He summed up this kind of lifestyle in the exhortation to "love one another" (1:5), a clear reference to the great commandments of Jesus—to love God and love your neighbor (Matthew 22:36–40; John 13:34).

In other words, those who walk in the truth should be people who love others. But they should be cautious whom they love. Deceivers and false teachers had infiltrated the church—people who taught falsehoods about the person of Jesus, teaching that He was not truly a man but only appeared to be one. This early heresy, called Docetism, required the strongest possible response from John. So the apostle warned the true believers away from these false teachers. John's encouragement, then, was not simply to love but to love others within the limits that truth allows.

How Do I Apply This?

John's strong encouragement to the believers in 2 John involved loving one another. However, John did not leave love undefined but described it as walking "according to His commandments" (2 John 1:6). This echoes the teaching of Jesus in John's gospel, where the Lord told His followers, "If you love Me, you will keep My commandments" (John 14:15).

Our love is dependent on our obedience. When we don't obey, we don't love. Often we get in the mind-set that our obedience to God affects only ourselves. But that simply is not true. Our actions, whether obedient or disobedient, have ripple effects far beyond our own limited vision of a circumstance.

Consider your own life. In what ways might your obedience or disobedience impact those in your immediate circle of relationships? Second John reminds us not only of the dangers of falling away from the truth but also of the importance of making obedience a priority in our lives—for ourselves and for those most important to us.

SECOND JOHN

	Introduction	Walk in Truth and Love!	Stand against Error!	Conclusion
	Greeting Affirmation Encouragement	The lady's children The lady herself Love one another; walk in obedience	The circumstance (many deceivers) The warning ("Watch yourselves!") The instruction (strong but necessary)	Personal Farewell
	VERSES 1–3	*VERSES 4–6*	*VERSES 7–11*	*VERSES 12–13*
Emphasis	Encouragement to love and affirm		Exhortation to be discerning	
Tone	Gracious	Concerned	Strong	Warm
Personal Touch	I love you (1:1)	"I ask you" (1:5)	I warn you (1:8)	"I hope to come to you" (1:12)
Theme		Loving others within the limits that truth allows		
Key Verses		1:5–6		
Christ in 2 John		Jesus, the Son of the Father, is the only way to the Father (1:3, 9).		

THIRD JOHN

Who Wrote the Book?

The apostle John identified himself in 3 John only as "the elder" (3 John 1:1), the same as he did in 2 John. At the writing of this, his final epistle, John was nearing the end of his life, a life that had changed dramatically some six decades before, when Jesus had called John and his brother James out from their fishing boat. The boys had left their livelihood and their father Zebedee to follow Jesus (Matthew 4:21–22). While James was the first of the twelve disciples to die for his faith, John outlived all the others. John referred to himself in his gospel as "the disciple whom Jesus loved" (John 21:20), a title that highlights one of the great themes of all John's biblical contributions, including 3 John— the love of God working itself out in the lives of human beings.

Where Are We?

While we cannot pinpoint the date with certainty due to the lack of specific information in the letter, 3 John was probably written around AD 90 from the island of Patmos, where John was exiled at the time. John wrote his letter to Gaius, a leader of one or more churches in Asia Minor. The apostle had received a report of some difficulties caused by a man named Diotrephes, and John wrote to reinforce for Gaius the proper way to deal with the troubles.

Why Is Third John so Important?

While Gaius was dealing with certain troubles in his area, John wanted to direct him, not only in how to respond to the trials but also how to relate to those who proclaim the truth. John's three epistles are largely concerned with the issue of fellowship—with God, with enemies of the gospel and, in the case of 3 John, with those who proclaim the truth. John wanted to ensure a warm welcome from the churches to those who traveled around preaching the gospel, offering them hospitality and a send-off "in a manner worthy of God" (3 John 1:6).

What's the Big Idea?

Troubles had come to the church in Asia. Diotrephes had taken control of one of the churches there and used his power to ban certain travelling missionaries from coming to the church at all. At one point, the church had seen something of a leadership quality in him and had placed him in charge, but now in the top spot, the power had gone to his head. He refused to welcome those traveling ministers of the gospel to preach and take rest with his church. And even worse, upon receiving an earlier correction from John, Diotrephes refused to listen (3 John 1:9).

This troubling situation prompted John to write to Gaius, commending the believers for holding fast to the truth and doing so with a loving attitude. These Christians strove to make the gospel a reality in their lives through the way they treated one another. And John, in response to this good report about the behavior of these "rank and file" Christians, encouraged them to continue to love and support those visiting believers who gave of themselves and ministered in the churches of Asia.

How Do I Apply This?

How do you show hospitality to other Christians, particularly those who serve you and others in your local church and at churches around the world? Showing hospitality to others—particularly strangers—requires a level of trust and acceptance that is not necessarily required of us in our everyday lives. It forces us to rely on a common bond in Jesus Christ, rather than a particular blood relationship or shared experience. It forces us out of our comfort zones and into a territory where we must place our trust in God.

John used words such as *love* and *truth* to describe this kind of living, and he used the negative example of Diotrephes to illustrate the dangers of going down a different path. We have a responsibility as Christians to live according to the truth we find in the life and ministry of Jesus, to care for and support those who serve God's people. Our Lord was surrounded by people who took care of Him. Third John teaches us that we should do the same for those who carry on the teaching of Jesus in our own day.

THIRD JOHN

	Encouragement of Gaius	Confrontation of Diotrephes	Affirmation of Demetrius	Conclusion
	Sickly (?)	Proud	Good testimony	Letter is abbreviated
	Obedient	Rigid and negative	Community	John hopes to visit
	Hospitable	Accusing	Scriptures	Shalom!
	Loving	"Church boss" complex	John	
	Supportive			
	VERSES 1–8	VERSES 9–11	VERSE 12	VERSES 13–14
Tone	Confirming	Denunciating	Endorsing	
Relationships	To the truth of God	With other Christians	In the world	
Emphasis	Keep it up!	Stop it!	Good for you!	
Paraphrase	I love you, and I pray for you (1:1–2)	I call attention to your deeds (1:10)	I hear good things about him (1:12)	
Theme	Holding to the truth with a loving attitude			
Key Verse	1:11			
Christ in 3 John	Jesus is the Name, for whose sake believers minister (1:7–8).			

JUDE

—— ✣ ——

Who Wrote the Book?

Like most of the other general epistles, the title of this little book takes its name from its author. Most scholars identify the writer as Jude the half-brother of Jesus for at least two reasons. First, he identified himself as the "brother of James" (Jude 1:1), meaning he was probably not the apostle named Jude, a man who was called "the son of James" (Luke 6:16). That the author of the book of Jude identified himself as the brother of James likely aligns him with the family of Jesus. (See "Who Wrote the Book" in the chapter on James for more information.) Second, Matthew 13:55 records the names of the brothers of Jesus as James and Judas. Whereas the gospels record his name as Judas, English translations shorten it to Jude—probably for the same reason no one in the present day wants to name a child Judas, because of the association it has with Judas Iscariot, the disciple who betrayed Jesus.

Like his older brother James, Jude did not place his faith in Jesus while the Lord was still alive. Only after the crucifixion and resurrection did the scales fall from Jude's eyes and he become a follower of his half-brother, Jesus. First Corinthians 9:5 offers a tantalizing piece of information, noting that the Lord's brothers and their wives took missionary journeys. From this scant portrait, we begin to picture Jude as a man who lived in skepticism for a time but eventually came to a powerful faith in Jesus. And as he traveled on behalf of the gospel—telling the story in city after city with his name Judas butting up against that of Judas Iscariot—he would stand as a living example of faithfulness, a stark contrast to the betrayer.

Where Are We?

The book of Jude is notoriously difficult to date, primarily because the Bible and tradition reveal so little about the personal details of its author while the book itself refrains from naming any particular individuals or places. The one clue available to present-day readers is the striking similarity between the books of Jude and 2 Peter. Assuming Peter wrote his letter first (AD 64–66), Jude probably wrote his epistle sometime between AD 67 and 80.

Why Is Jude so Important?

Jude's edgy brevity communicates the urgency of his notion that false teachers needed to be condemned and removed from the church. Few words meant that Jude would not waste space dancing around the issue. He saw within the church people and practices that were worthy of condemnation, including rejecting authority and seeking to please themselves. In response to these errors, Jude marshaled much biblical imagery to make clear what he thought of it all—anything from Cain killing his brother Abel to the punishment of the sinful people who populated Sodom and Gomorrah (Jude 1:7, 11).

What's the Big Idea?

Jude's purpose in his letter was twofold: he wanted to expose the false teachers that had infiltrated the Christian community, and he wanted to encourage Christians to stand firm in the faith and fight for the truth. Jude recognized that false teachers often peddled their wares unnoticed by the faithful, so he worked to heighten the awareness of the believers by describing in vivid detail how terrible dissenters actually were. But more than simply raising awareness, Jude thought it important that believers stand against those working against Jesus Christ. Believers were to do this by remembering the teaching of the apostles, building each other up in the faith, praying in the Holy Spirit, and keeping themselves in the love of God (Jude 1:17, 20–21).

How Do I Apply This?

Fight for the truth! Stand up against error! The book of Jude is the very definition of punchy and pithy proclamations—with its short commands and statements popping off the page like machine-gun fire. But in our day and age, punchy has become rude or unacceptable. In many circles the forcefulness of Jude will not be tolerated, the crowds preferring a softer and gentler side of the Christian faith. But Jude reminds us that there is a time and a place for the aggressive protection of the truth from those who would seek to tear it down.

How can you participate in defending the truth from error?

JUDE

	Greeting and Purpose	Exposure of False Teachers	Warnings and Commands to Christians	Benediction
	Mercy, peace, and love **What to do:** Contend for the faith! **Why:** Certain persons have secretly slipped in.	Doom is certain Guilt is sure Spirituality is empty Lives are godless	"Remember!" (1:17) "Keep yourselves!" (1:21) "Have mercy!" (1:22) "Save!" (1:23)	Our ultimate hope Our infinite God
	VERSES 1–4	*VERSES 5–16*	*VERSES 17–23*	*VERSES 24–25*
Emphasis	Appealing	Revealing	Reminding	Praising
Tone	Personal concern	Bold exposure	Strong exhortation	Great hope
Directed to	Those "beloved in God the Father" (1:1)	Those who "indulged in gross immorality" (1:7)	"But you, beloved . . ." (1:17, 20)	"The only God" (1:25)
Theme	Exposing false teachers and standing firm in the faith			
Key Verses	1:3, 21–23			
Christ in Jude	Jesus is our only Master and Lord, who will judge the false prophets at His coming (1:4, 14–16).			

THE
APOCALYPSE

Revelation, also known as the Apocalypse, has long been regarded as one of the most difficult biblical books to interpret. It stands out in a number of ways: it is the only New Testament book to deal primarily with prophetic events; it is couched in symbolic language; and it records some of the most disturbing and difficult imagery in the entire Bible. These elements have created a deep divide among scholars in regard to interpreting the particulars of the book. However, its message of hope to the faithful remains undeniable.

REVELATION

Who Wrote the Book?

The author of Revelation mentioned his name, John, four times throughout the book (Revelation 1:1, 4, 9; 22:8). Christians throughout history
have given almost unanimous affirmation to the identity of the book's
author as John the apostle, who had been exiled to the island of Patmos
by the authorities for preaching the gospel in Asia. Some traditions say
that the Romans dropped John into a vat of boiling oil, but when the
apostle did not die, they instead banished him to the barren rock of
Patmos.

The title of the book, Revelation, comes from the Greek word for
apocalypse and refers to an unveiling or a disclosure of something as yet
unknown. This title is certainly appropriate for the book, a work so
interested in making known the events of the future.

Where Are We?

The apostle John wrote the book of Revelation around the year AD 95
from his exile on the island of Patmos. He addressed his work to seven
Asian churches — Ephesus, Smyrna, Pergamum, Thyatira, Sardis,
Philadelphia, and Laodicea. Because John worked in Ephesus for so
many of his later years, it would have been natural for him to
communicate this vision to the churches under his immediate care and
influence. Each of those seven churches received a message directed
specifically to them (chapters 2 and 3) before John launched into his
account of the future which he received in his vision from God.

Why Is Revelation so Important?

The book of Revelation provides the clearest biblical portrait of the events of the tribulation, dealing with the specifics of that terrible time (chapters 4–18). The tribulation will be a time of judgment, a time when those left on the earth after the rapture will suffer deeply for their nonbelief. John pictured this judgment as a series of twenty-one events—inaugurated by the breaking of seven seals, the blowing of seven trumpets, and the pouring out of seven bowls. This grand judgment on the sinfulness of humanity shows the seriousness with which God views sin—payment will be exacted from those not covered by the blood of Jesus Christ.

What's the Big Idea?

While Revelation offers many details on the tribulation—even if they are often couched in the mystery of symbolic language—it is the final four chapters that dictate the overall message of the book. Revelation 19–22 portrays Christ's future triumph over the forces of evil and His re-creation of the world for the redeemed. Ultimately, the book—and the world—end in a final victory for truth and goodness and beauty.

For the bulk of its sixty-six books, the Bible portrays a world deep in the throes of suffering. Human beings have had a problem with sin since the fall in Genesis 3, and verse after verse has recorded our problem in painstaking detail. The brilliance of Revelation is that it provides a final answer to this problem, a hope that Jesus will once and for all heal the wounds wrought by sin (Revelation 19), reign for a thousand years on earth (Revelation 20), and then re-create the world into a place that represents God's original design (Revelation 21–22). The Bible's narrative is a simple one: creation, fall, re-creation. Without the completion of the redeeming work of Jesus recorded in Revelation, we wouldn't have the end of the story, leaving our hope for the future in serious doubt.

How Do I Apply This?

Usually when people mention the book of Revelation, they immediately think about judgment. And without a doubt, much judgment occurs in the book. However, Revelation does not end with judgment. Instead, it provides a striking bookend for the entire Bible, which begins in Paradise and ends in Paradise. More than judgment on the evildoers, Revelation is a book about hope for the faithful in Christ.

What pains or indignities have you suffered? What broken relationship have you wept over? Has death's sword struck deep into your heart? Revelation promises a world where pain and tears and death pass away. Revelation reminds us that there is indeed hope beyond the momentary trials and struggles of this life. One day the darkness will pass away, and we will all dwell in perpetual light.

Come quickly, Lord Jesus! God be praised.

REVELATION

"I am the Alpha . . ." (1:8) . . . and the Omega" (22:13)

	"The things which you have seen . . ."	"The things which are . . ."	"The things which will take place." (Revelation 1:19)
	Personal and biographical	Christ's letters to the seven churches	Christ as Judge (chapters 4–5) The tribulation (chapters 6–18) The coming of Christ (chapter 19) The millennium (chapter 20) The eternal state (chapters 21–22)
	CHAPTER 1	CHAPTERS 2–3	CHAPTERS 4–22
Scope	History: looking back		Prophecy: looking ahead
Style	Dialogue		Observations and questions
Scene	On earth		Shifts between earth and heaven
Theme	Christ's future triumph over the forces of evil and His re-creation of the world for the redeemed		
Key Verses	1:7, 19; 22:12–13		
Christ in Revelation	Jesus is the coming King of Kings and Lord of Lords, who will return as Judge and King to usher in the kingdom of God on earth (19:11–20:6).		

APPENDIXES

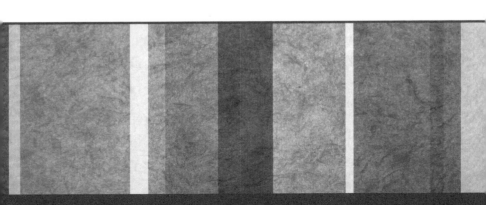

JESUS'S MINISTRY IN ISRAEL

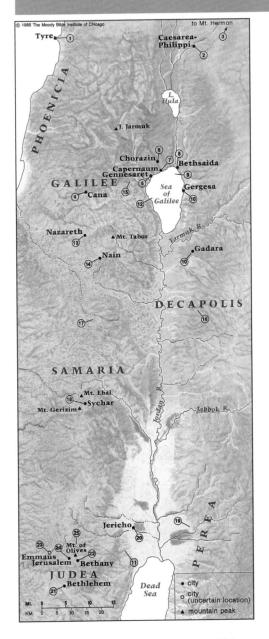

© 1985 The Moody Bible Institute of Chicago

It is impossible to definitively arrange events in the life of Jesus chronologically; hence the present arrangement follows a geographic axis, basically in a north-to-south order. Because the first gospel book most frequently contains information cited here, synoptic passages are keyed to the book of Matthew, except where not attested there or where more pertinent documentation is available in another gospel.

1. Region of Tyre: Syrophoenician woman's daughter healed—Matthew 15:21–28.

2. Caesarea-Philippi: Peter's great confession—Matthew 16:13–20.

3. Mount Hermon: (a) possible location of Transfiguration—Matthew 17:1–13; (b) epileptic boy healed nearby—Matthew 17:14–21.

4. Cana of Galilee: (a) water changed to wine—John 2:1–11;
(b) Capernaum official's son healed—John 4:46–54.

5. Gennesaret: many healings—Mark 6:53–56.

6. Area of Chorazin: (a) judgment pronounced on cities of Chorazin, Bethsaida, and Capernaum—Matthew 11:20–24; (b) possible area of Sermon on the Mount—Matthew 5–7.

Continued on next page

121

JESUS'S MINISTRY IN ISRAEL (CONTINUED)

7. Capernaum: (a) draught of fishes—Luke 5:1–11; (b) demoniac healed—Mark 1:21–28; (c) Sermon on the Mount—Matthew 5–7; (d) Peter's mother-in-law healed—Matthew 8:14–15; (e) centurion's servant healed—Matthew 8:5–13; (f) paralytic healed—Mark 2:1–12; (g) woman with issue of blood healed—Mark 5:25–34; (h) Jairus's daughter raised—Luke 8:40–56; (i) two blind men healed—Matthew 9:27–31; (j) mute demoniac healed—Matthew 9:32–34; (k) man with withered hand healed—Matthew 12:9–13; (l) blind and mute demoniac healed—Matthew 12:22–37; (m) tribute provided—Matthew 17:24–27; (n) Bread of Life discourse—John 6:22–59.

8. Bethsaida: (a) location of feeding of multitudes—Matthew 14:13–21; Matthew 15:32–39; (b) blind man healed—Mark 8:22–26.

9. Sea of Galilee near Bethsaida: walking on water—Matthew 14:22–33.

10. Gergesa/Gadara: possible location of casting out demons, which entered swine, the swine then rushed down a steep bank and drowned—Luke 8:26–39.

11. Wilderness: temptation—Matthew 4:1–11.

12. Sea of Galilee: storm quieted—Matthew 8:23–27.

13. Nazareth: (a) boyhood home—Matthew 2:19–23; (b) rejected by townspeople—Luke 4:16–30.

14. Nain: widow's son raised—Luke 7:11–17.

15. Galilee: (a) leper cleansed—Mark 1:35–45; (b) post-resurrection appearances—Matthew 28:16–20; see also John 21:1–22; 1 Corinthians 15:7 (disciples).

16. Decapolis: many healings—Matthew 15:29–31; Mark 7:31–37.

17. Between Galilee and Samaria: ten lepers healed—Luke 17:11–19.

18. Sychar: woman at well of Samaria—John 4:1–42.

19. Perea: (a) teachings on marriage—Matthew 19:1–12; (b) possible location of healing of woman with infirmity—Luke 13:10–13; (c) possible location of healing of man with dropsy—Luke 14:1–6.

20. Jericho: (a) Bartimaeus healed—Mark 10:46–52; (b) Zacchaeus converted—Luke 19:1–10.

21. Bethlehem: birthplace—Luke 2:1–20.

22. Bethany: Lazarus raised—John 11:1–44.

23. Emmaus: post-resurrection appearance—Luke 24:13–32 (two men).

24. Jerusalem: (a) discourse with Nicodemus—John 3:1–21; (b) Pool of Bethesda healing—John 5:2–9; (c) woman caught in adultery—John 8:2–11; (d) attempted stoning—John 8:12–59; (e) man blind from birth healed—John 9:1–12; (f) Passion Week (see map of Jesus's Final Days in Jerusalem on next page); (g) post-resurrection appearances—John 20:1–18 (Mary Magdalene), 20:19–31 (with and without Thomas).

25. Mount of Olives: (a) Olivet discourse—Matthew 24:3–25:46; (b) ascension—Acts 1:6–12.

JESUS'S FINAL DAYS IN JERUSALEM

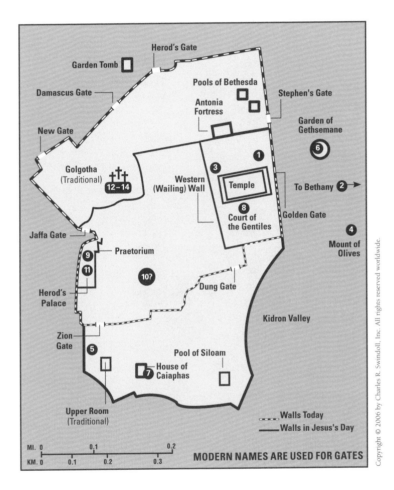

Herod's Gate

Garden Tomb

Damascus Gate

Pools of Bethesda

Antonia Fortress

Stephen's Gate

New Gate

Garden of Gethsemane **6**

Golgotha (Traditional) **12–14**

Western (Wailing) Wall

3   **1**

Temple

To Bethany **2**

8

Court of the Gentiles

Golden Gate

Jaffa Gate

4

Mount of Olives

9

Praetorium

11

10?

Herod's Palace

Dung Gate

Kidron Valley

Zion Gate

5

Pool of Siloam

House of Caiaphas **7**

Upper Room (Traditional)

Walls Today
Walls in Jesus's Day

MI. 0   0.1   0.2
KM. 0   0.1   0.2   0.3

MODERN NAMES ARE USED FOR GATES

SUNDAY

1. Jesus descended from Bethany and entered the temple precincts.

SUNDAY NIGHT

2. Jesus returned to Bethany to lodge with His friends.

Continued on next page

JESUS'S FINAL DAYS
IN JERUSALEM (CONTINUED)

MONDAY

3. Jesus cleansed the temple (Mark 11:15; Luke 19:45–47).

TUESDAY

4. Jesus taught His disciples on the Mount of Olives about the end times (Matthew 26:30; Mark 14:26–33; Luke 22:39).

THURSDAY

5. Jesus shared the Passover meal with His disciples in the Upper Room (Matthew 26:17–29; Mark 14:10–25; Luke 22:7–38; John 13:3–15).

6. Jesus retired to Gethsemane with His disciples. Jesus prayed, the disciples slept, Judas betrayed Him, and Jesus was arrested (Matthew 26:36; Mark 14:32; John 18:1).

THURSDAY/FRIDAY

7. Jesus was taken to the high priests Annas and Caiaphas for a preliminary hearing (Matthew 26:57–68; 27:1; Mark 14:53; Luke 22:54; John 18:12–13, 24).

8. Jesus was taken before the Sanhedrin (Matthew 27:1).

FRIDAY

9. Jesus appeared before Pilate, the governor (Matthew 27:2, 11–14; Mark 15:1; Luke 23:1; John 18:38).

10. Jesus appeared before Herod Antipas (Luke 23:6–12).

11. Jesus appeared before Pilate a second time (Matthew 27:15–26; Luke 23:18–25; Mark 15:6–15; John 18:39–19:16).

12. Jesus was crucified on Golgotha, "The Place of the Skull" (Matthew 27:31–50; Mark 15:22–37; Luke 23:33–44; John 19:17–30).

13. Jesus was buried in Joseph of Arimathea's tomb (Matthew 27:60; Mark 15:46; Luke 23:53; John 19:38).

EARLY SUNDAY MORNING

14. Jesus appeared to Mary at the tomb after He arose (John 20:11–18).

PAUL'S FIRST AND SECOND MISSIONARY JOURNEYS

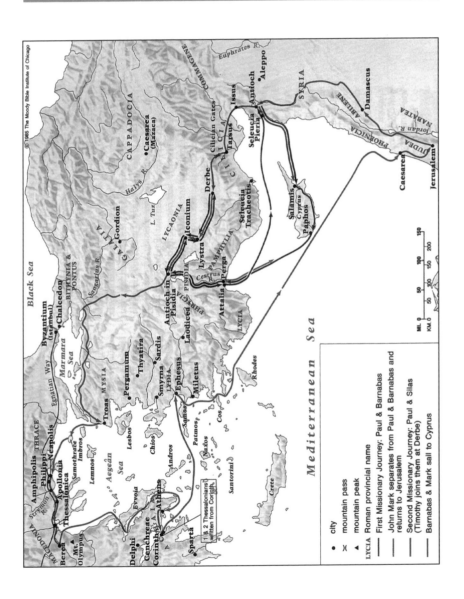

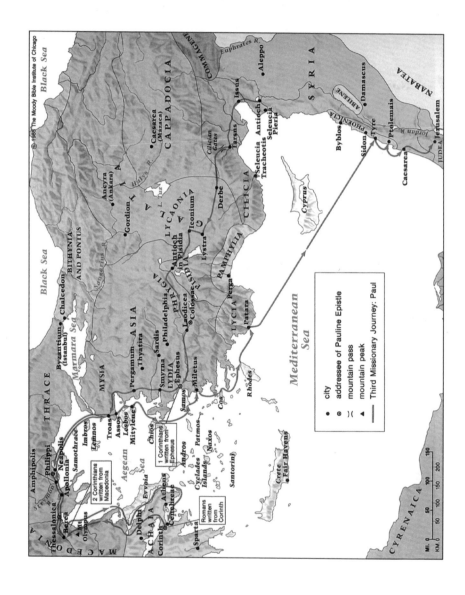

PAUL'S THIRD MISSIONARY JOURNEY

PAUL'S JOURNEY TO ROME

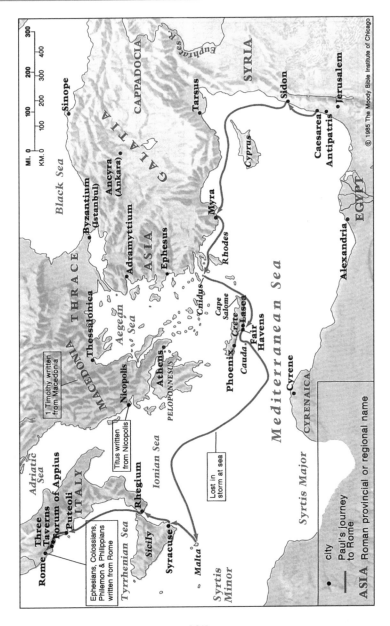

TIMELINE OF NEW TESTAMENT BOOKS AND EVENTS

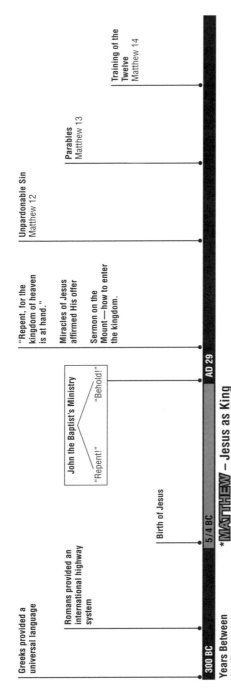

PREPARATION FOR THE CHRIST

OFFER OF THE CHRIST

ANTICIPATION OF THE REJECTION OF THE CHRIST

Greeks provided a universal language

Romans provided an international highway system

Birth of Jesus

John the Baptist's Ministry

"Repent!"   "Behold!"

"Repent, for the kingdom of heaven is at hand."

Miracles of Jesus affirmed His offer

Sermon on the Mount—how to enter the kingdom.

Unpardonable Sin
Matthew 12

Parables
Matthew 13

Training of the Twelve
Matthew 14

Years Between the Testaments

300 BC

5/4 BC

AD 29

*MATTHEW – Jesus as King
MARK – Jesus as Servant
LUKE – Jesus as Son of Man
JOHN – Jesus as Son of God

Legend: GOSPELS • HISTORY • *Pauline Epistles* • *General Epistles* • The Apocalypse

*The Gospels and the book of Acts are placed in the timeline where their events occurred.
The Epistles and the Apocalypse are placed where they were written.

TIMELINE OF NEW TESTAMENT BOOKS AND EVENTS, CONT.

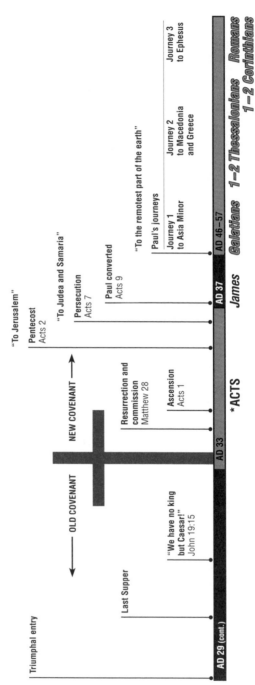

PRESENTATION AND REJECTION OF THE CHRIST

PROCLAMATION OF CHRIST BY THE CHURCH

Triumphal entry

Last Supper

"We have no king but Caesar!"
John 19:15

← OLD COVENANT

NEW COVENANT →

Resurrection and commission
Matthew 28

Ascension
Acts 1

"To Jerusalem"

Pentecost
Acts 2

"To Judea and Samaria"

Persecution
Acts 7

Paul converted
Acts 9

"To the remotest part of the earth"

Paul's journeys

Journey 1
to Asia Minor

Journey 2
to Macedonia and Greece

Journey 3
to Ephesus

AD 29 (cont.)

AD 33

AD 37

AD 46–57

*ACTS

James

Galatians 1–2 Thessalonians Romans
1–2 Corinthians

Legend: GOSPELS • HISTORY • Pauline Epistles • General Epistles • The Apocalypse
*The Gospels and the book of Acts are placed in the timeline where their events occurred.
The Epistles and the Apocalypse are placed where they were written.

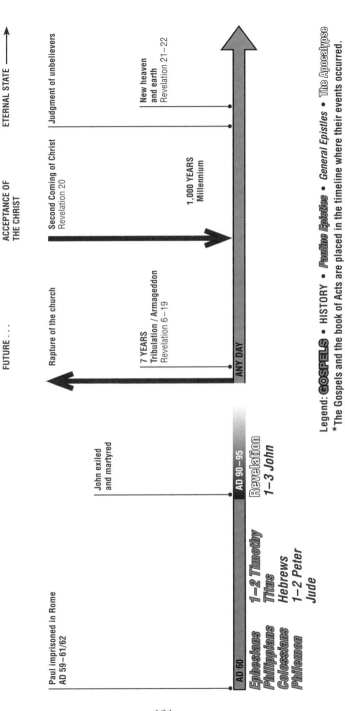

TIMELINE OF NEW TESTAMENT BOOKS AND EVENTS, cont.

FUTURE. . .

ACCEPTANCE OF
THE CHRIST

ETERNAL STATE ⟶

Paul imprisoned in Rome
AD 59–61/62

John exiled
and martyred

Rapture of the church

Second Coming of Christ
Revelation 20

Judgment of unbelievers

New heaven
and earth
Revelation 21–22

7 YEARS
Tribulation / Armageddon
Revelation 6–19

1,000 YEARS
Millennium

ANY DAY

AD 60

AD 90–95

Ephesians
Philippians
Colossians
Philemon

1–2 Timothy
Titus
Hebrews
1–2 Peter
Jude

Revelation
1–3 John

Legend: GOSPELS • HISTORY • *Pauline Epistles* • *General Epistles* • The Apocalypse
*The Gospels and the book of Acts are placed in the timeline where their events occurred.
The Epistles and the Apocalypse are placed where they were written.

THE LIFE OF JESUS

Please reference the map on page 121 for locations listed in the charts.
(All events are listed in chronological order.)

BIRTH AND YOUTH		
Jesus born	Luke 2:1–20	Bethlehem
Jesus named and circumcised at eight days	Luke 2:21	Bethlehem
Jesus presented in the temple	Luke 2:22	Jerusalem
Wise men visit Jesus	Matthew 2:1–12	Bethlehem
Escape to Egypt	Matthew 2:13–18	Egypt
Jesus grows up in Nazareth	Matthew 2:23	Nazareth
Jesus, age 12, goes to the temple for Passover	Luke 2:41–42	Jerusalem
BAPTISM AND EARLY MINISTRY		
Jesus baptized	Mark 1:9–11	Jordan River
Jesus's temptation by Satan	Matthew 4:1–11	Wilderness
First miracle: wedding in Cana	John 2:1–11	Cana
Jesus stays in Capernaum	John 2:12	Capernaum
Passover: cleansing the temple	John 2:13–22	Jerusalem
Nicodemus comes to Jesus at night	John 3:1–21	Jerusalem
Jesus and the woman at the well	John 4:4–26	Region of Samaria
Jesus returns to Galilee	John 4:43–45	Galilee
MINISTRY IN GALILEE		
Jesus heals the nobleman's son	John 4:46–54	Cana
Jesus rejected by the people	Luke 4:16–30	Nazareth
Jesus calls the fishermen	Matthew 4:18–22	Beside the Sea of Galilee
Jesus heals a leper	Matthew 8:2–4	Galilee
Jesus heals a paralytic	Matthew 9:1–8	Capernaum

Continued on next page

133

MINISTRY IN GALILEE (continued)		
Jesus calls Matthew	Matthew 9:9	Capernaum
Parables about fasting	Matthew 9:14–17	Capernaum
Questions about the Sabbath	John 5:1–18	Jerusalem
Controversies	Matthew 12	Galilee
Jesus appoints the Twelve	Mark 3:13–19	Galilee
Sermon on the Mount	Matthew 5:1–8:1	Galilee
Jesus forgives the sins of the adulterous woman	Luke 7:36–50	Galilee
Jesus stills the storm	Mark 4:35–41	Sea of Galilee
Jesus heals Jairus's daughter	Mark 5:21–24, 35–43	Beside the Sea of Galilee
Jesus heals the woman with an issue of blood	Mark 5:25–34	Beside the Sea of Galilee
Jesus heals the blind and the demon-possessed	Matthew 9:27–34	Galilee
Jesus rejected at Nazareth	Matthew 13:54–58	Nazareth
WITHDRAWAL FROM GALILEE		
Jesus feeds five thousand people	Matthew 14:13–21	Near Bethsaida
Jesus walks on water	Matthew 14:24–33	Sea of Galilee
Jesus rejected in Capernaum	John 6:24, 41–66	Capernaum
Pharisees criticize disciples for eating with unclean hands	Mark 7:1–8	Capernaum
Jesus feeds four thousand people	Matthew 15:32–38	Beside the Sea of Galilee
Pharisees and Sadducees ask Jesus for a sign	Matthew 16:1–4	Dalmanutha
Jesus heals a blind man	Mark 8:22–26	Bethsaida
Peter's confession of Christ	Matthew 16:13–20	Near Caesarea Philippi
Jesus predicts His death and resurrection	Matthew 16:21	Near Caesarea Philippi
The transfiguration	Matthew 17:1–8; Luke 9:28	Mount Hermon (probably)

Continued on next page

WITHDRAWAL FROM GALILEE (continued)		
Jesus refers to His death and resurrection	Matthew 17:22–23	Galilee
Jesus pays tax with money retrieved from a fish	Matthew 17:24–27	Capernaum
Jesus teaches about forgiveness	Matthew 18:15–35	Capernaum
Jesus rebukes James and John	Luke 9:51–56	Between Samaria and Galilee
MINISTRY IN JUDEA		
Jesus celebrates the Feast of Tabernacles	John 7:10–53	Jerusalem
Jesus says He is God's Son	John 8:31–59	Jerusalem
Parable of the good shepherd	John 10:1–18	Jerusalem
Jesus sends out the Seventy	Luke 10:1	Judea
Parable of the good Samaritan	Luke 10:25–37	Judea
Jesus visits Mary and Martha	Luke 10:38–42	Bethany
Jesus at the Feast of the Dedication	John 10:22–39	Jerusalem
MINISTRY IN PEREA		
Many believe in Jesus	John 10:40–42	Perea
Requirements of a disciple	Luke 14:25–35	Perea
Jesus raises Lazarus from the dead	John 11:1–44	Bethany
Jesus heals ten lepers	Luke 17:11–19	Between Samaria and Galilee
Jesus meets Zaccheus	Luke 19:1–10	Jericho
THE MIRACLES OF JESUS		
Turning water into wine	John 2:1–11	Cana
Healing an official's son	John 4:46–54	Cana
First miraculous catch of fish	Luke 5:1–11	Sea of Galilee
Delivering a demoniac in the synagogue	Mark 1:21–28	Capernaum
Healing Peter's mother-in-law	Matthew 8:14–15	Capernaum

Continued on next page

135

THE MIRACLES OF JESUS (continued)		
Cleansing a leper	Luke 5:12–16	Galilee
Healing a paralytic	Matthew 9:1–8	Capernaum
Healing an infirm man at the Pool of Bethesda	John 5:1–15	Jerusalem
Healing a man's withered hand	Luke 6:6–11	Galilee
Healing a centurion's servant	Matthew 8:5–13	Capernaum
Raising a widow's son	Luke 7:11–17	Nain
Stilling a storm	Mark 4:35–41	Sea of Galilee
Healing a woman with a hemorrhage	Mark 5:25–34	Beside the Sea of Galilee
Raising Jairus's daughter	Luke 8:41–56	Beside the Sea of Galilee
Healing two blind men	Matthew 9:27–31	Galilee
Casting out a spirit that kept a man from speaking	Matthew 9:32–34	Galilee
Feeding the five thousand	John 6:1–14	Near Bethsaida
Walking on the water	Mark 6:45–52	Sea of Galilee
Casting out a demon from a Syrophoenician's daughter	Mark 7:24–30	Near Tyre and Sidon
Healing a blind man of Bethsaida	Mark 8:22–26	Bethsaida
Casting out a demon from an insane boy	Matthew 17:14–21	Mount Hermon
Finding money in a fish's mouth	Matthew 17:24–27	Capernaum
Healing a man born blind	John 9:1–7	Jerusalem
Casting out a spirit that kept a man from speaking	Luke 11:14–26	Judea (probably)
Healing a woman infirmed for eighteen years	Luke 13:10–17	Judea
Healing a man with dropsy	Luke 14:1–6	Perea
Raising Lazarus	John 11:1–44	Bethany
Cleansing ten lepers	Luke 17:11–19	Between Samaria and Galilee

Continued on next page

THE MIRACLES OF JESUS (continued)		
Healing blind Bartimaeus	Mark 10:46–52	Jericho
Cursing a fig tree	Matthew 21:18–19	Jerusalem
Healing Malchus's ear	Luke 22:49–51	Gethsemane
Second miraculous catch of fish	John 21:1–14	Sea of Galilee
TRIALS AND CRUCIFIXION **(See details on page 123–124.)**		
RESURRECTION AND ASCENSION		
Resurrection and the empty tomb	Matthew 28:1–7	Jerusalem
Jesus appears to Mary Magdalene	John 20:11–18	Jerusalem
Jesus appears on the road to Emmaus	Luke 24:13–35	Emmaus
Jesus appears to the Eleven	Luke 24:36–49	Jerusalem
Jesus appears to Thomas	John 20:24–29	Jerusalem
Jesus appears by the Sea of Galilee	John 21	Sea of Galilee
Jesus appears to more than five hundred at one time	1 Corinthians 15:6	Galilee
Jesus challenges witnesses to reach the world	Acts 1:8	Mount of Olives
Jesus ascends into heaven	Acts 1:3–11	Mount of Olives

CHRONOLOGY OF THE NEW TESTAMENT BOOKS

Book	Author	Approximate Date AD	Place of Composition	Roman Emperor
James	James	45–48	Jerusalem	Claudius
Galatians	Paul	48	Antioch	Claudius
1 Thessalonians	Paul	51	Corinth	Claudius
2 Thessalonians	Paul	51	Corinth	Claudius
1 Corinthians	Paul	55	Ephesus	Nero
2 Corinthians	Paul	56	Philippi?	Nero
Romans	Paul	57	Corinth	Nero
Mark	Mark	57–59	Rome?	Nero
Luke	Luke	58–60	Rome?	Nero
Ephesians	Paul	60	Rome	Nero
Colossians	Paul	60–61	Rome	Nero
Philemon	Paul	60–61	Rome	Nero
Acts	Luke	60–62	Rome?	Nero
Matthew	Matthew	60–65	Judea or Syria?	Nero
Philippians	Paul	61–62	Rome	Nero
1 Timothy	Paul	63	Macedonia	Nero
Titus	Paul	63	Nicopolis	Nero
1 Peter	Peter	64	Rome	Nero
2 Peter	Peter	64–66	Rome	Nero
Hebrews	Unknown	64–68	Unknown	Nero
2 Timothy	Paul	67	Rome	Nero
Jude	Jude	67–80	Unknown	Nero–Vespasian
John	John	85–95	Ephesus?	Domitian
1 John	John	90	Patmos	Domitian
2 John	John	90	Patmos	Domitian
3 John	John	90	Patmos	Domitian
Revelation	John	95	Patmos	Domitian

THE FASCINATING BACKDROP OF THE NEW TESTAMENT

A little context, please!

The message of the New Testament comes into brighter view when we understand the times in which it was written. The decade of the AD 60s was the most prolific season for the writing of the New Testament books. Paul's Prison Epistles, the gospel of Matthew, Peter's letters, and the letter to the Hebrews were all penned between AD 60 and 68, most written from Rome, the capital of the world at the time. What was that contemporary world like? In a word: *shaky.*

Keep in mind that during these years of crises, the letters of Peter (from Rome) and the letter to the Hebrews encouraged the "Followers of the Way" to cast all their cares on God and to continue in the faith.

DATE AD	FACT
63	On the morning of **February 5, 63**, an **earthquake** measuring 6.4 on the Richter scale rattled the Mediterranean basin, specifically ravaging southern Italy and the city of Pompeii.
64	On the night of **July 18, 64**, a **fire** broke out among the shops lining the Circus Maximus, Rome's massive chariot stadium. The flames raged for six days before coming under control; then the fire reignited and burned for another three. When the smoke cleared, ten of Rome's fourteen districts were in ruin.
68	The **political tensions heated up** on **June 9, 68**, when psychopathic Emperor Nero, who had had the apostles Paul and Peter executed, was forced by his political adversaries to kill himself.

Continued on next page

DATE AD	FACT (*continued*)
69	The year **AD 69** is known as the year of the **four emperors**. Nero was succeeded by Galba who was murdered by Otho in **January 69**. Otho committed suicide on **April 16**, avoiding death by Vitellius, who was beheaded on **December 20** by Vespasian, who finally established a new dynasty.
70	Across the Mediterranean, the Roman armies declared their five-month **siege of Jerusalem** complete with the destruction of Herod's Temple on **September 7, 70**.
73	On **April 16, 73**, after a three-year standoff with the Romans on the tabletop rock plateau of Masada in the Judean wilderness, having fled the destruction of Jerusalem in AD 70, 960 people in the Sicarii community preferred **death by suicide** over surrender to the Romans.
79	Rounding out two tumultuous decades, on the afternoon of **August 24, 79**, a volcano in central southern Italy, **Mount Vesuvius, erupted**, destroying Pompeii, Herculaneum, and other Roman cities.

Galatians 4:4 says that in the fullness of time, God sent His Son. Fully aware of the events and people that would be on the scene, God chose the first century to be the backdrop of the earthly life of Christ, the writing of the New Testament books, and the spread of Christianity to the world.

Appendix D

READING THE OLD TESTAMENT ANEW

If you're a lover of God's Word, you can come to appreciate and value the treasures you mine from the Old Testament. Whether it's an increased understanding of Old Testament history, insight into God's grace or holiness, or the application of a significant moral principle, the Old Testament has much to offer the believer in Christ. In addition to the historical, theological, and ethical principles we draw from the Old Testament itself, the New Testament provides additional insight into the reading of the Bible's first thirty-nine books. Observing the way New Testament authors cite the Old Testament is both enlightening and instructive as we each seek to be informed readers of the entire Bible.

An Authoritative Reading

All of the New Testament authors believed in the authority of the Old Testament—it was their Bible. The New Testament writers pictured God as the author of the Old Testament (Matthew 15:4–6), associated Scripture with the very words of God (Romans 9:17), and portrayed God as speaking through an Old Testament saint or prophet (Mark 12:36; Acts 28:25). Even without quoting the Old Testament, Jesus would base an entire argument on its authority (John 8:17). In the end, it is clear that the New Testament authors, as well as Jesus Himself, presumed the authority of the Old Testament—it truly revealed the mind and will of God to His people.

A Paraphrased Reading

Have you ever stumbled across an Old Testament quotation in the New, flipped back to Isaiah or Psalms to find the quote in its original context, and been surprised to find the two quotes not matching up? Why does that happen? Did the New Testament authors just misquote the Old Testament? Did they have a bad copy? Or is there something else going on? A couple of significant points can account for the differences.

First, New Testament authors were often either translating the Hebrew Bible into Greek or quoting from the already completed Greek translation of the Old Testament, called the Septuagint. Occasionally the Septuagint simplifies the Hebrew or interprets it, meaning that quotations will not quite match up, such as in the difference between Isaiah 52:5 and Romans 2:24. Second, the New Testament authors lived at a time when documentation standards were quite different than today's—for instance, they used no quotation marks. They also paraphrased regularly and often alluded to a text, rather than offer a word-for-word quotation.

We often summarize verses today—listen carefully to your pastor on Sunday or to your own words when talking about Scripture. You will find yourself saying things like, "Scripture says, 'God loved the world and sent His Son so that people who believe in Him can have eternal life.'" An exact quote of John 3:16? Of course not. But those words are certainly in the spirit of the verse, just as the New Testament authors kept the spirit of the Old Testament verses they referenced. And remember, the Spirit of God was guiding them.

A Christological Reading

Finally and most important, the New Testament authors read their Old Testaments in light of their theological commitments and beliefs, especially in light of the person and work of Jesus Christ. Under the inspiration of the Holy Spirit, they often took single verses beyond their historical or prophetic context and applied them to particular theological truths. The best example of this is in Romans 3:10–18, where Paul took six different verses or passages from the Psalms and Isaiah and strung them together to make a point about the fallen state of humanity. Paul was not concerned at the moment with the original purpose of, say, Psalm 14 or Isaiah 59, but with its contribution to New Testament theology. Preachers today do this all the time when they present topical sermons. The topic of Paul's sermon in Romans 3? Sin.

More than working out general theological topics though, New Testament authors applied the Old Testament to the life and ministry of Jesus. They often emphasized single verses as reflective of some truth about Christ. For example, Matthew 2:15 makes reference to Hosea 11:1, a verse that in its original context referred to Israel. As used by Matthew, Hosea 11:1 predicts the return of God's Son, Jesus, from His hiding place in Egypt. John 19:36 follows the same pattern in citing Psalm 34:20. While in the psalm David wrote generally about the righteous, John in his gospel recognized a clear reference to the crucifixion. These are only two examples of a regular pattern throughout the New Testament, a pattern that should earn our consideration as we seek to become better readers of Scripture.

In the end, the New Testament teaches us a great deal about reading the Old Testament. It is important to read the New and the Old Testaments in their historical context — these events actually happened. However, the New Testament shows us that reading the Bible — even the Old Testament — through a christological lens is absolutely essential. We have not properly understood Scripture until we read it in light of Jesus Christ. As the linchpin of Christianity, Jesus stands at the center of Scripture. Let's make sure He stays there.

AFTER THE NEW TESTAMENT
What Happened to the Apostles?

While the New Testament hints at the deaths of some of the apostles (Mark 10:38–39; John 21:18–19; 2 Timothy 4:6–7), none of their deaths are actually recorded in the Bible except for that of James, the brother of John (Acts 12:1–2). We know the resurrection of Jesus changed their lives dramatically, as they followed His direction to share the gospel throughout the world (Acts 1:8). But what happened to them after the short history that the Bible records? Where did they go and how did they die? Church tradition has passed down their stories, which portray committed men who followed the command of Jesus to go and share the good news, not just for a few years but faithfully for the rest of their lives.[1]

- **James**, son of Zebedee and brother of John the apostle, ministered in Jerusalem immediately after the resurrection of Jesus. A man turned in James to the authorities because of the apostle's Christian faith. When the accuser saw the result of the apostle's death sentence, he was moved to become a Christian himself. They were beheaded together in Jerusalem, possibly as soon as AD 36 (Acts 12:1–2).

- **Thomas**, the apostle who doubted Jesus and then believed (John 20:24–28), ministered to the east of Israel, traveling as far as Persia (modern-day Iran) and even into India. While in India, he met his end with a poisoned dart.

- **Simon the Zealot** preached in both Mauritania, located in West Africa, and in Britain. He was eventually crucified for his faith.

- **Bartholomew** traveled east from Israel, preaching as far as India and even translating the gospel of Matthew into the native language there. Eventually, while he was serving in Armenia, the people beat him to death with staffs and beheaded his dead body.

- **Andrew**, brother of Peter, went north from Israel to preach in Scythia (modern-day Ukraine, Russia). He then made his way to the city of Patras in Achaea (located in modern-day southern Greece), where he was crucified on an X-shaped cross because he counted himself unworthy to die on a cross like the one that held Jesus.

- **Matthew**, the tax collector and gospel writer, preached the gospel in Ethiopia and Egypt. Since Matthew won many converts, the Egyptian king had him run through with a spear.

- **Philip**, who preached to the Ethiopian eunuch (Acts 8:26–40), preached primarily in the area of Asia Minor (modern-day Turkey) and Greece. He was crucified and stoned to death in the city of Hierapolis, located in southern Asia Minor.

- **James**, son of Alphaeus, preached the gospel in Egypt, where he was clubbed to death.

- **Jude**, also known as Thaddeus, preached throughout the Middle East in Judea, Samaria, Syria, and Edessa. He was martyred by beating in the city we now know as Beirut, Lebanon.

- **Peter**, brother of Andrew, ministered in Rome during the persecution of Christians by Nero. The emperor set out to capture Peter, who willingly surrendered to martyrdom. He was crucified upside down, probably in AD 66–68.

- **Paul**, the great apostle to the Gentiles, had been imprisoned in Rome for his faith. Government officials escorted him to the site of his beheading on the outskirts of Rome, most likely in AD 67.

- **John**, brother of James, ministered for many years in Jerusalem and then in Ephesus. He was exiled for a time on the island of Patmos under the reign of Domitian and likely died in Ephesus of natural causes when he was 100 years old, around AD 95–100.

While many of their deaths were grisly, the martyrdoms of the apostles should strike Christians as anything but depressing. Even today, some two thousand years after they met their demise, the apostles provide an encouraging and invigorating model of commitment to Jesus Christ. May their examples of making the ultimate sacrifice for our Lord spur us on to lives of greater faithfulness in the face of our own trials and tribulations.

HOW TO BEGIN A RELATIONSHIP WITH GOD

The New Testament tells the story of Jesus Christ—the divine Son of God who came to earth, took on human flesh, lived a sinless life, died on the cross, and was raised again on the third day, all for the sake of bringing human beings back into right relationship with our Creator. If you're interested in having a right relationship with God, receiving forgiveness for your sins and transformation into the Creator's ideal for His creation, the Bible marks the path to salvation with four essential truths. Let's look at each marker in detail.

Our Spiritual Condition: Totally Depraved

The first truth is rather personal. One look in the mirror of Scripture, and our human condition becomes painfully clear:

> "There is none righteous, not even one;
> There is none who understands,
> There is none who seeks for God;
> All have turned aside, together they have become
>   useless;
> There is none who does good,
> There is not even one." (Romans 3:10–12)

We are all sinners through and through—totally depraved. Now, that doesn't mean we've committed every atrocity known to humankind. We're not as *bad* as we can be, just as *bad off* as we can be. Sin colors all our thoughts, motives, words, and actions.

You still don't believe it? Look around. Everything around us bears the smudge marks of our sinful nature. In spite of our best efforts to create a perfect world, crime statistics continue to soar, divorce rates keep climbing, and families keep crumbling.

Something has gone terribly wrong in our society and in our-selves—something deadly. Contrary to how the world would repackage it, "me-first" living doesn't equal rugged individuality and freedom; it equals death. As Paul said in his letter to the Romans, "The wages of sin is death" (Romans 6:23)—our spiritual and physical death that comes from God's righteous judgment of our sin, along with all of the emotional and practical effects of this separation that we experience on a daily basis. This brings us to the second marker: God's character.

God's Character: Infinitely Holy

How can God judge each of us for a sinful state we were born into? Our total depravity is only half the answer. The other half is God's infinite holiness.

The fact that we know things are not as they should be points us to a standard of goodness beyond ourselves. Our sense of injustice in life on this side of eternity implies a perfect standard of justice beyond our reality. That standard and source is God Himself. And God's standard of holiness contrasts starkly with our sinful condition.

Scripture says that "God is Light, and in Him there is no darkness at all" (1 John 1:5). God is absolutely holy—which creates a problem for us. If He is so pure, how can we who are so impure relate to Him?

Perhaps we could try being better people, try to tilt the balance in favor of our good deeds, or seek out methods for self-improvement. Throughout history, people have attempted to live up to God's stan-dard by keeping the Ten Commandments or living by their own code of ethics. Unfortunately, no one can come close to satisfying the demands of God's law. Romans 3:20 says, "By the works of the Law no flesh will be justified in His sight; for through the Law comes the knowledge of sin."

Our Need: A Substitute

So here we are, sinners by nature and sinners by choice, trying to pull ourselves up by our own bootstraps to attain a relationship with our holy Creator. But every time we try, we fall flat on our faces. We can't live a good enough life to make up for our sin, because God's standard isn't "good enough"—it's *perfection*. And we can't make amends for the offense our sin has created without dying for it.

Who can get us out of this mess?

If someone could live perfectly, honoring God's law, and would bear sin's death penalty for us—in our place—then we would be saved from our predicament. But is there such a person? Thankfully, yes!

Meet your substitute—*Jesus Christ*. He is the One who took death's place for you!

> [God] made [Jesus Christ] who knew no sin to be sin on our behalf, so that we might become the righteousness of God in Him. (2 Corinthians 5:21)

God's Provision: A Savior

God rescued us by sending His Son, Jesus, to die on the cross for our sins (1 John 4:9–10). Jesus was fully human and fully divine (John 1:1, 18), a truth that ensures His understanding of our weaknesses, His power to forgive, and His ability to bridge the gap between God and us (Romans 5:6–11). In short, we are "justified as a gift by His grace through the redemption which is in Christ Jesus" (3:24). Two words in this verse bear further explanation: *justified* and *redemption*.

Justification is God's act of mercy, in which He declares righteous the believing sinners while we are still in our sinning state. Justification doesn't mean that God *makes* us righteous, so that we never sin again, rather that He *declares* us righteous—much like a judge pardons a guilty criminal. Because Jesus took our sin upon Himself and suffered our judgment on the cross, God forgives our debt and proclaims us PARDONED.

Redemption is Christ's act of paying the complete price to release us from sin's bondage. God sent His Son to bear His wrath for all of our sins—past, present, and future (Romans 3:24–26; 2 Corinthians 5:21). In humble obedience, Christ willingly endured the shame of the cross for our sake (Mark 10:45; Romans 5:6–8; Philippians 2:8). Christ's death satisfied God's righteous demands. He no longer holds our sins against us, because His own Son paid the penalty for them. We are freed from the slave market of sin, never to be enslaved again!

Placing Your Faith in Christ

These four truths describe how God has provided a way to Himself through Jesus Christ. Because the price has been paid in full by God, we must respond to His free gift of eternal life in total faith and confidence in Him to save us. We must step forward into the relationship with God that He has prepared for us—not by doing good works or by being a good person but by coming to Him just as we are and accepting His justification and redemption by faith.

> For by grace you have been saved through faith; and that not of yourselves, it is the gift of God; not as a result of works, so that no one may boast. (Ephesians 2:8–9)

We accept God's gift of salvation simply by placing our faith in Christ alone for the forgiveness of our sins. Would you like to enter a relationship with your Creator by trusting in Christ as your Savior? If so, here's a simple prayer you can use to express your faith:

> *Dear God,*
>
> *I know that my sin has put a barrier between You and me. Thank You for sending Your Son, Jesus, to die in my place. I trust in Jesus alone to forgive my sins, and I accept His gift of eternal life. I ask Jesus to be my personal Savior and the Lord of my life. Thank You. In Jesus's name, amen.*

If you've prayed this prayer or one like it and you wish to find out more about knowing God and His plan for you in the Bible, contact us at Insight for Living. Our contact information is on the following pages.

WE ARE HERE FOR YOU

If you desire to find out more about knowing God and His plan for you in the Bible, contact us. Insight for Living provides staff pastors who are available for free written correspondence or phone consultation. These seminary-trained and seasoned counselors have years of experience and are well-qualified guides for your spiritual journey.

Please feel welcome to contact your regional Pastoral Ministries by using the information below:

United States
Insight for Living
Pastoral Ministries
Post Office Box 269000
Plano, Texas 75026-9000
USA
972-473-5097, Monday through Friday,
8:00 a.m. – 5:00 p.m. central time
www.insight.org/contactapastor

Canada
Insight for Living Canada
Pastoral Ministries
Post Office Box 2510
Vancouver, BC V6B 3W7
CANADA
1-800-663-7639
info@insightforliving.ca

Australia, New Zealand, and South Pacific
Insight for Living Australia
Pastoral Care
Post Office Box 443
Boronia, VIC 3155
AUSTRALIA
1 300 467 444

United Kingdom and Europe
Insight for Living United Kingdom
Pastoral Care
PO Box 553
Dorking
RH4 9EU
UNITED KINGDOM
0800 915 9364
+44 (0)1306 640156
pastoralcare@insightforliving.org.uk

ENDNOTES

What Makes the New Testament New?

1. Bill Cosby, *Kids Say the Darndest Things* (New York: Bantam Books, 1999), 22–23.

Luke

1. Helmut Koester, *Ancient Christian Gospels: Their History and Development* (Harrisburg, Pa.: Trinity Press International, 1990), 335. (Accessed on Google Books, March 25, 2010.)

Acts

1. Helmut Koester, *Ancient Christian Gospels: Their History and Development* (Harrisburg, Pa.: Trinity Press International, 1990), 335. (Accessed on Google Books, March 25, 2010.)

Appendix E
After the New Testament: What Happened to the Apostles?

1. You can find the list of Jesus's twelve disciples in Luke 6:13–16 (see also Matthew 10:2–4 and Mark 3:16–19). James (the half-brother of Jesus) and Paul are not included in these biblical lists because they became apostles after the death and resurrection of Jesus. Paul famously met the risen Lord on the road to Damascus (Acts 9:1–9).

RESOURCES FOR PROBING FURTHER

To further your study of the New Testament, we recommend the following resources. Of course, we cannot always endorse everything a writer or ministry says, so we encourage you to approach these and all other nonbiblical resources with wisdom and discernment.

Bailey, Mark, and Tom Constable. *The New Testament Explorer: Discovering the Essence, Background, and Meaning of Every Book in the New Testament.* Nashville: Thomas Nelson, 1999.

Barker, Kenneth L., and John R. Kohlenberger III, eds. *The Expositor's Bible Commentary: New Testament.* Abridged ed. Grand Rapids: Zondervan, 2004.

Beitzel, Barry J. *The Moody Atlas of Bible Lands.* Chicago: Moody Press, 1985.

House, H. Wayne. *Chronological and Background Charts of the New Testament.* 2nd. ed. Grand Rapids: Zondervan, 2009.

Jensen, Irving L. *Jensen's Survey of the New Testament.* Chicago: Moody Publishers, 1981.

Pentecost, J. Dwight. *The Words and Works of Jesus Christ: A Study of the Life of Christ.* Grand Rapids: Zondervan, 2000.

Radmacher, Earl D., Ronald B. Allen, and H. W. House, eds. *Nelson's New Illustrated Bible Commentary: Spreading the Light of God's Word into Your Life.* Nashville: Thomas Nelson, 1999.

Swindoll, Charles R. *Swindoll's New Testament Insights: Insights on John.* Grand Rapids: Zondervan, 2010.

Swindoll, Charles R. *Swindoll's New Testament Insights: Insights on Romans.* Grand Rapids: Zondervan, 2010.

Swindoll, Charles R., and John F. Walvoord. *'Til His Kingdom Comes: Living in the Last Days*. Plano: Insight for Living, 2007.

Tenney, Merril C., ed. *Zondervan's Pictorial Bible Dictionary*. Grand Rapids: Zondervan, 1999.

Walvoord, John F., and Roy B. Zuck, eds. *The Bible Knowledge Commentary: New Testament*. Wheaton, Ill.: Victor Books, 1983.

Wiersbe, Warren W. *The Wiersbe Bible Commentary: New Testament*. Colorado Springs: David C. Cook, 2007.

Yancey, Philip. *The Jesus I Never Knew*. Grand Rapids: Zondervan, 2002.

ORDERING INFORMATION

If you would like to order additional copies of *Insight's New Testament Handbook: A Practical Look at Each Book* or order other Insight for Living resources, please contact the office that serves you.

United States

Insight for Living
Post Office Box 269000
Plano, Texas 75026-9000
USA
1-800-772-8888 (Monday through Friday,
7:00 a.m.–7:00 p.m. central time)
www.insight.org
www.insightworld.org

Canada

Insight for Living Canada
Post Office Box 2510
Vancouver, BC V6B 3W7
CANADA
1-800-663-7639
www.insightforliving.ca

Australia, New Zealand, and South Pacific

Insight for Living Australia
Post Office Box 443
Boronia, VIC 3155
AUSTRALIA
1 300 467 444
www.insight.asn.au

United Kingdom and Europe

Insight for Living United Kingdom
PO Box 553
Dorking
RH4 9EU
UNITED KINGDOM
0800 915 9364
www.insightforliving.org.uk

Other International Locations

International constituents may contact the U.S. office through our Web site (www.insightworld.org), mail queries, or by calling +1-972-473-5136.